FRONTIER
BOULDER

RICHARD FETTER

Johnson Books: Boulder

For Joel and Scott, in hopes that some day they will come to enjoy the history of the place where they were born.

Cover: Design by Joseph Daniel, color tinting by Margaret Lignitz

Cover illustration: Boulder Creek (*Our Native Land*, George T. Ferris, 1886)

© 1983 by Richard Fetter

ISBN 0-933472-72-2

Printed in the United States of America by Johnson Publishing Company
1880 South 57th Court
Boulder, Colorado 80301

Contents

Acknowledgements

Special thanks to Cassandra Volpe and the staff at the University of Colorado, Western History Collection; Ellen Wagner and Leanne Sander of the Boulder Historical Society; and Lois Anderton, Librarian/Archivist of the Boulder Public Library, Carnegie Branch. Their kind, professional assistance has been very much appreciated.

PART I
The Mountains Looked Right

Red Rocks and Green Rocks

In June of 1912, the *Boulder Daily Camera* carried a story headlined "Aunty Brookfield is Ninety-One, Hale, Hearty And Jovial As Ever." Accompanied by the photograph of a bespectacled, austere-looking pioneer woman, the story told how Mrs. Brookfield came out west in the spring of 1859 and was, as far as is known, the first white woman to set foot upon the land which would become the site of Boulder, Colorado.

Born in Augusta, Georgia, Aunty Brookfield had moved west to Illinois with her father, then crossed the plains to Iowa and ultimately Nebraska City. There she met and married Alfred A. Brookfield, a twenty-eight year-old grocer who became mayor of Nebraska City in 1857.

In the spring of 1858 rumors began drifting back from the mountains that gold had been discovered around Auraria and Cherry Creek. Leaving his wife behind, Brookfield joined a party under Captain Thomas A. Aikens, a fifty year-old Missouri farmer, and headed west to strike it rich. The party made its way across the plains, following the Platte River to Fort Kearney and Ogallala before turning southwest along the South Platte River to Julesburg and beyond. Where St. Vrain Creek joins the river, the men came to the ruins of old Fort St. Vrain, a crumbling relic of the fur trading days.

Eighteen years later Captain Aikens described the moment: "I mounted the walls . . . and with my field glass could see that the mountains looked right for gold; could see bands of Indian ponies and bands of deer and antelope grazing close up to the high foot-hills; could see that the valley . . . was the loveliest of all the valleys in the scope of vision—a landscape exceedingly beautiful. Those moun-

Captain Thomas A. Aikens, the Missouri farmer who led a party of gold seekers to the site of Boulder in October 1858. (From Bixby, *History of Clear Creek and Boulder Valleys*)

tains are so high and steep, the boys said, that it will not be safe to venture up till Spring, on account of snow slides. But the following morning was so fair, and the love of adventure and hope of gold so inviting, that we forded the Platte and traveled up, with the bold mountains all before us, till we pitched our tents under the red rock cliff, near where the Red Rock flouring mill now is, at the mouth of Boulder Canon."

"The mountains looked right for gold." The words are legendary in Boulder's past, but we can pause to wonder to what extent Aikens' memory was dimmed by the passage of time. When these words were quoted in the *Boulder County News* in 1876, Captain Aikens was a respected citi-

A. A. Brookfield joined the Aikens party and became one of Boulder's first settlers. In February 1859 he helped form a company to "lay out and commence to build what may be an important town." (From Bixby, *History of Clear Creek and Boulder Valleys*)

zen of Boulder, an elder statesman of the town, and, above all, one of its true pioneers. But if you drive out U.S. 85 today and head north toward Greeley, the mountains become quite distant by the time you reach Gilcrest, a small town near the site of old Fort St. Vrain.

Adventure, yes. Beauty, of course. Both could beckon, for the unusual shapes of the Flatirons are readily discernible from here with a high-powered lens, although forty miles away. But to say that "the mountains looked right for gold" sounds a little like a prominent man sitting back in his chair, warming up to a good story. Aikens, like Brookfield and almost everyone else who came out in search of gold knew next to nothing about how to find it or where. They might have guessed that the gold in Cherry Creek had to wash down from somewhere, but even then they couldn't have known whether streams ran out of the mountains above Boulder and into Cherry Creek.

Whatever the compulsion, the grocer and the farmer led their party up the St. Vrain to its Boulder branch, eventually arriving at the mouth of Boulder Canyon. Years later some recalled seeing the light of sunset on the northernmost Flatiron. Since this view is seen more readily from the area around Sunshine Canyon, there has been some speculation that the first settlers camped there rather than at the mouth of Boulder Canyon. If you go to Settlers Park today, however, you have only to walk up the hill toward Red Rocks to gain a view of the northernmost Flatiron. The men could easily have camped at the mouth of Boulder Canyon, as they said they did, and remembered the sunset on the Flatirons from walks up the hill. In any event, on October 17, 1858, the Aikens party was here. The men pitched their tents and settled in to look for gold. Because of the red sandstone cliffs, they called the place Red Rocks, giving Boulder its first name. Unknown to any of them, they had just become the first permanent white settlers in the Boulder valley.

Red Rocks, which gave Boulder its first name, remains unchanged today from when the Aikens-Brookfield party arrived and camped nearby. (*Richard L. Fetter*)

Unfortunately, they may not have been the first white people to see this area. Six years earlier another party seems to have arrived, carrying out the final scenes in a tragedy that was all too typical of the early days of the West. According to an account written by A.C. Patton in 1904, his grandfather was crossing the plains in 1852 with a large party that included a family named Snodgrass. John Snodgrass and his wife, Mary, had one daughter, Josephine, who was known in camp as "Gyp" or "Gypsie," because of her streaming black hair and dark eyes. The wagons crossed the plains without incident as far as Julesburg. Somewhere beyond, on June 13, they were following a new trail apparently made by a large buffalo herd when a calf sprang from the grass, startling Gyp's pony. A chase began, and Gyp, despite her father's shouts, was soon half a mile in front of the wagon train with her father driving his wagon at full speed a quarter of a mile behind.

Rifle shots rang out and Indians appeared, grabbing the reins from Snodgrass. Gyp stopped at the sounds and was immediately surrounded by Indians. When the rest of the party caught up, Gyp was gone, her mother was dead, and her father was stunned by a ball which had pierced his scalp. Upon regaining consciousness an hour later, Snodgrass set out across the sandhills to rescue Gyp. They followed the trail to Old Fort Morgan and continued west for three more days until they reached what seems to be the area of South Boulder, for years later they described with great accuracy the "barren rocks" above "the coal camp of Marshall."

The following day the men saw smoke a few miles away near a formation of rocks that was almost green in color. The rescue party was within 500 yards of the green rocks when they heard a scream and saw Gyp rush down the mountain toward the rocks. She disappeared into a small opening, and an Indian appeared to seal off her escape. When the men got within rifle distance, the Indians saw that they couldn't recapture Gyp, and one of them shot an arrow into the opening between the rock walls. Snodgrass shot the Indian, and the rest of the Indians disappeared into the mountains.

Snodgrass reached his daughter only to find she had been pierced by an arrow, and she died in his arms. The men said a prayer, and while Snodgrass carried Gyp's body away Patton's grandfather carved the name "Gyp" on the entrance to the passageway in the rock. Following the descriptions given in his grandfather's letter, Patton went to the green rocks "across the gulch from where the great Sanitarium [Memorial Hospital] now stands" and took a picture of his grandfather's carving on "Gyp Rock," which he included with his publication.

Gyp Rock. If the story of Gyp is true, this carving in Knollwood would be the earliest evidence of whites in Boulder. (*Richard L. Fetter*)

Gold

For a time it seemed that the Aikens party wouldn't fare any better than poor Gyp. According to a history of Boulder County written by Amos Bixby in 1880, the party was soon visited by Left Hand, the Southern Arapahoe chief, who told them, "Go away; you come to kill our game, to burn our wood, and to destroy our grass."

Bear Head, another Arapahoe, was even more adamant. Referring to the comet that was then visible in November 1858, he asked, "Do you remember when the stars fell?"

"1833," the men said.

"That is right," Bear Head replied. "It was that year white man first came. And," he continued, referring again to the comet, "do you know what that star with a pointer means? The pointer points back to when the stars fell as thick as the tears of our women shall fall when you come to drive us away." Bear Head then gave the whites three days to leave the country, but when he returned he told them he had dreamed that Boulder Creek had flooded, swallowing up his people while the white people were saved. Then he went away.

Bixby's account told how Left Hand "fully intended to drive the white men off, but was caught by their guile" when the "crafty goldseekers" fed and flattered him. Later newspaper stories ended with Bear Head slinking away, his bluff called. More recent study suggests that English-speaking Left Hand, whose life was devoted to peace with the whites, told the whites they could stay through the winter and that Aikens told Left Hand they had no intention of remaining permanently. As confirmed by the recollections of Mrs. David H. Nichols, whose husband would play a major role in Indian matters at Sand Creek in 1864, gold seekers of the early days had only one aim: get rich quick and get back to civilization.

In any event, Aikens and his men remained. They built a cabin at Red Rocks in November, then added a dozen more along what is now Pearl Street. The shelters were crude and basic, with sod roofs, doorways covered with blankets or skins, and no windows. The men turned up a little "color" in some of the streams, and on December 9, 1858, *The Nebraska Advertiser* of Brownville, Nebraska, reported that "A young man returned from the auriferous region of Western Nebraska [Boulder was then part of the Nebraska Territory] bringing samples of gold which he obtained with his own hands." Twenty days later the *Advertiser* said Nebraska gold had been sent to New York and found to be worth $20 an ounce." Still, only traces had been found.

Fortunately for the men, the winter of 1858-59 was extremely mild. There was little snow on the ground, and the men could work in their shirtsleeves, enjoying the clear, balmy weather that can come to Boulder in January. Able to prospect even in the middle of winter, Aikens, Colonel I.S. Bull, Charles Clouser, William Huey, W.W. Jones, and David Wooley climbed into the mountains and struck gold at what became Gold Hill on January 16, 1859. They named the spot Gold Run. About $100,000 worth would be taken out that first season. Whether lucky or astute, Captain Aikens had been correct: the mountains were right for gold.

But before such riches could be realized, snow and cold set in. Only ten days after the discovery, A.A. Brookfield wrote to his wife in Nebraska that the idea of coming to Boulder was "damned humbug" and others ought to abandon it. But by February 27, things were looking a little brighter. Brookfield wrote, "Dear Wife: . . . I am well satisfied that I can make at least five dollars per day. I am quite of the opinion that we have but just commenced finding what we came here for, and our discoveries are creating much excitement at all the settlements, and people are coming in every day. There are now here on the creek, over one hundred men; and we hear from numbers more that will soon be here. The gold which we find is of quite a different quality from any that has been found at other places, and what is called 'shot gold'—all that has been found in other places is 'scale or float gold.' "

Other discoveries followed rapidly. On March 4, a party discovered shot or nugget gold on St. Vrain Creek. They went down to Auraria and spent two or three hundred dollars on tools and provisions, paying their bills with gold. In May J.D. Scott discovered the first quartz vein. George Jackson and John Gregory made major discoveries near Black Hawk but kept quiet until warmer weather came so they could stake their claims.

Despite whatever threats or promises may have passed between the Indians and whites, and despite whatever intentions the gold seekers may have had about striking it rich and heading home, it was rapidly becoming obvious that a permanent settlement was desirable as a base of operations. The most logical and convenient spot was right at the base of the boulder-filled canyon where the mountains rose dramatically from the plains. Possibly, with so many people coming in, it might just be worthwhile to lay out a town and sell some lots to the newcomers.

On February 10, 1859, fifty-four men got together to create the constitution and bylaws of the Boulder City Town Company. Brookfield said, "We thought that as the weather would not permit us to mine, we would lay out and commence to build what may be an important town." Boulder was named for all the boulders that were lying around the area, and Brookfield saw the town as the "head of wagon navigation for the miners in the mountains."

According to the articles of incorporation, Boulder's first legal description began "at a forked Dead tree, On the Right-hand bank of Boulder Creek, About one mile from the mouth of the Canon and Running due East Two (2) miles . . . ." In all, "Twelve Hundred and Eighty Acres of Land lying in Boulder Creek" were to be acquired and held "by Pre-Emption or Otherwise" then to be surveyed and subdivided "in a manner suitable for a Town Site." The property was described as being located in St. Vrain's County, Territory of Nebraska.

The regulations governed all aspects of the town with a surprising thoroughness. The constitution and bylaws covered the powers of the officers, meetings, drawings of lots, and distribution of shares. There was even a strict building code requiring that cabins be of "hewed logs containing not less than 255 superficial square feet, in the clear; and with an Altitude of not less than 8½ feet, to the upper Edge of the Eave log." Buildings had to be completed within sixty days of the date of the article, streets were to be laid out due north and south and due east and west, alleys were to be twenty feet wide, and lots 50'x40' laid out north and south. Every person not a member of the company and wishing to erect a building upon the town site would be entitled to choose two inside lots and draw two or more at the drawing of the company. There were 100 lots in the original survey and fifty-four signers to the original document. Captain Aikens was elected president of the company.

On March 28, 1903, George R. Williamson, one of the original "58ers" recalled Boulder's first platting in *The Saturday Truth*, a small local publication:

"The first plat was of course a rude affair: it did not even take for the running of the lines a pocket compass of which every man possessed one. Exactly in the middle of the present intersection of Twelfth [Broadway] and Pearl Streets, a stick was driven and sighting across this stick to the black spur in the prairie, known as the Valmont Butte, Pearl Street, the main thoroughfare, was easily lined. The side streets were laid out at right angles with the aid of the same compass, but the main street stands today as then with its face directly toward the butte. . . ."

Pearl Street of course is still one of Boulder's main streets, but who Pearl was, or why the street was so named, may forever remain a mystery. On March 25, 1859, John L. Buell, W.B. Moore, and W.S. Buckwalter were chosen to number the blocks and lots in the company's holdings and to name the streets. A plat of the town site made in April 1859 shows Pearl Street, but the minutes of the meetings do not show the sources of the names. There are no records of a woman in Boulder by that name at that time. In fact, there were very few women around at all. On March 17, 1931, the *Daily Camera* said in a story about a Helen Teets of Denver that George Allen England of Philadelphia told her Pearl Street was named for his mother. Pearl England was the wife of an army man who surveyed in Colorado, but there is no evidence that he was in Boulder at the time or was even known by the early settlers. However, this may be as close as we ever come to identifying the mysterious Pearl, if indeed the name was for a woman at all.

It seems surprising that men of this era should try to set up a community with such rules and regulations governing their existence. Such a step refutes our images of the early days of the West as a time when people were free to wander

Pearl Street in 1885. Laid out with the aid of a stick and Valmont Butte, Pearl today remains one of Boulder's most important streets. (*Boulder Historical Society*)

a boundless land. There were no fences and no government. Colorado was years away from even considering statehood. "Colorado" didn't even exist yet. Why then would men decide to regulate themselves with so much apparent thoroughness?

The answers lay in security and order, and even the miners, whom we picture as the most hard-headed, hard-nosed and independent of any people in the West, set up constitutions and laws to govern their early mining districts. The fact is that the land which the miners and settlers were claiming, whether around Pike's Peak, Boulder, or elsewhere, was not theirs. According to the Kansas-Nebraska Act of 1854, it belonged to the Indians. Lacking government and a system of order, the miners, like the settlers in Boulder, banded together to create a self-governing community with power over all within its borders.

The first two mining districts were organized at Gold Hill and Boulder by the summer of 1859. The districts not only provided for the name, boundaries, officers and laws of the district, but went on in some instances to provide means for handling disputes, fees to be charged, and punishments.

With a perspicacity that undoubtedly would have its admirers today, some of the districts, like Sugarloaf, did not allow a lawyer to appear in a case in the district unless he was a party to the suit. In that case the opposite party was allowed to employ counsel. "Common law and substantial Justice shall be the rule of practice in all cases," declared the law in Ward. "No technicalities will be allowed to defeat the ends of justice."

Nor was there any softheartedness shown with regard to punishments. Murder was punished by hanging; perjury or theft was worth ten to twenty-five lashes on the bare back and banishment from the district and confiscation of property; salting a claim or destroying a landmark was worth $10-$50. Not paying a fine was worth ten to twenty-five lashes and banishment.

Of course it didn't work out in practice quite as well as it all sounded. Claims and lot sites were jumped, and miners' meetings often disintegrated into chaos.

One letter from Jamestown told how a meeting began with the singing of "Sweet Betsy From Pike." The purpose of the meeting was to determine "the opening of the lots held by speculators to actual settlers." Pandemonium broke out and up to six people started speaking at once until a motion was made to keep still and address the delicate matter of whether "a lot had actually been sold for a keg of beer." One of the "best of men" stated, "We have no doubt a lot had been sold for a keg of beer, but the beer was drunk, and drunk or sober the title was just as good as if the consideration had been money."

Subsequently, two men had a fight over a lot and the one that drew "first blood" held the lot. "Now," the letter continued, "the talk is to call another miners' meeting and make it a law that 'first blood' shall hold against all other titles. We want your candid opinion—is first blood a good title?"

While such issues were being hotly debated in the mountains, the speculators of the Boulder City Town Company were trying their best to make Boulder work. On March 5, 1859, they petitioned the Governor of the Territory of Ne-

Emma "Aunty" Brookfield, one of the seventeen women at the Christmas Eve dance in 1859. Fifty years later she reigned as queen of Boulder's semicentennial celebration. (From Bixby, *History of Clear Creek and Boulder Valleys*)

braska for a charter for the city. Five days later they moved to have a post office at Boulder City.

The problem was that they were asking the exorbitant price of $1000 a lot. With nearby government land available at $1.25 an acre, the venture was doomed to fail. Nevertheless, Boulder City continued to make its first crude beginnings. A few cabins went up on the north side of Boulder Creek, and the town center began to form around the intersection of Twelfth and Pearl.

It took until the end of 1859 before there was a whipsawed board floor in town, and a dance was held on Christmas Eve to commemorate the event. Two hundred men were in attendance and all seventeen of the ladies, including Aunty Brookfield, who had come out to join her husband that spring.

Even with one board floor around, Boulder's crude log buildings offered only the simplest of shelters. We have a rare glimpse of what the first cabins were like from the recollections of Mrs. David H. Nichols, who arrived in

Boulder in the summer of 1860: "Having friends already located here we immediately drove to their cabin. We found it to be a room about eighteen by twenty feet. It was made of logs, with one small window, one door, a dirt floor and a "shake" roof.

"The shakes were measured about three feet in length and were made of strips split from logs. They were laid on in much the same way that shingles are but instead of being nailed were held in place by poles notched and fastened to the top logs of the cabin by wires. Nails were too hard to obtain and too expensive to be used only where very necessary.

"In the east of this room was a small fireplace, the lower part of which was made of rocks held in place by clay—as no one then knew the location of the limestone bed west of town. The upper portion or chimney proper was made of sticks laid tier upon tier and plastered over with mud to prevent their catching on fire.

"On the south side of the room was the bed-stead made of poles one end of which was hewn off and driven into the wall, while the other end was fastened into a post in the same manner. Poles were also used for slats. This bed-stead was

The early cabins were crude affairs. (*Boulder Historical Society*)

at least three feet from the floor, so that the space beneath could be used for a sort of store-room.

"By the time I had placed upon it a large bag called a tick, well stuffed with grass, and upon that a good sized featherbed which we had brought from our home in Illinois, my husband was often obliged to help me into bed in much the same manner that he assisted me to mount my mustang.

"On the opposite side of the cabin two pegs were driven in the wall, and upon these pegs was a board made by hand with the aid of a rip-saw, which served as a table. As that later luxury, a dry goods box, had not arrived."

There was also a table "with legs of different sizes, cut from pieces of pole with the bark still on them. The top was made of a piece split out of a large log and hewn off until it was reasonably smooth. This served as a work table."

The remainder of the furniture consisted of three three-legged top heavy stools that tipped over easily and a Franklin stove the Nicholses had brought with them across the plains. Most of their neighbors had to get by with either a sheet iron stove or bake ovens and reflectors which did not keep an even heat. The Nicholses also enjoyed the luxury of an elbow and a joint of pipe that enabled them to obtain sufficient draft to keep the fire burning and prevent the stove from smoking.

As she later recalled, Mrs. Nichols spent many a day "baking bread from six o'clock in the morning until ten or twelve at night. For bread with meat, beans, dried apples, milk and butter was about all the food we early settlers had." Eggs were a luxury and vegetables were available only in summer. Water had to be carried from the creek for all household purposes except doing the laundry, which was done at the creek. This lasted until the fall of 1860 when the town well was dug. Even then "many settlers continued to take their laundry wash-boilers and tubs down to the banks of the stream where they built fires, heated water, and washed their soiled clothing. And visited with their neighbors and any newcomers who had arrived since the last wash-day."

Two months after the Nicholses arrived in June 1860, J.W. Partridge built a shingle mill. One day, with the aid of about forty men who had come down from the mountains for supplies, Nichols shingled his house, the first in Boulder, while Mrs. Nichols prepared dinner for all.

"Lightning Express—Root Hog or Die"

Horace Greeley passed through Boulder in June 1859 and described it as a "log hamlet of some thirty habitations." In August Rev. J. Adriance arrived and found Boulder to be a collection of "10-12 log houses, none completed." Yet, in February John L. Buell had said 60-75 houses were being built.

The apparent inconsistency is explained to a large extent by the fact that, as the months went by, the search for easy riches gave way to the realities of rough living conditions and hard luck. Discouraged, many people moved their homes from the town to try their luck on the outlying farms.

Part of the problem was sheer ignorance. "They thought that they would only have to dig in the sands for a few weeks in order to make themselves rich for life," wrote Mrs. Nichols of the "wondrous fairy tales told about gold" and the people who bounced across the plains in prairie schooners chasing their dreams. Once they arrived they dashed off to the mountains, thoroughly untrained, pick in hand, trying here and there at random in hopes of making a lucky strike. But as one gold seeker wryly cracked, "The only thing I took out of South Boulder was Peabody. He fell in and came near being drowned."

John A. Hitchings was typical of the many who toiled long and hard but mostly in vain. The grandson of a man who had fought at Bunker Hill, Hitchings arrived in Gold Hill in August 1859 at age thirty-nine. Almost forty years later he wrote an autobiographical sketch recalling how he "found some 300 men had mined at Gold Hill all summer but the water was about gone when I came to stop late in August. I had my wife's brother with me and some tools and supplies, hardly sufficient to last until winter. We built a cabin, whip-sawed some lumber, shot an elk, but did not get any gold until next spring. . . . Flour sold at $20 to $36 per 100 lbs, and other things in proportion."

"Think of his life," wrote Nathaniel Hill of Henry Blake, who had mines at Sugarloaf in 1864. "For more than four years he has lived nearly alone in the mountains. Sometimes for two months he has not seen a human being. He became satisfied early that he was in a rich mineral district, and was determined not to leave it until he could make his fortune. One discouragement after another has met him. It seems quite probable now that his hopes will be realized. His cabin was constructed of logs roofed with shingles which he split with an axe. The beds, of which there were two, one above the other, were made by driving posts in the ground, fastening stretchers to them by willow withes, and then laying on cross pieces. Over these, hay was spread. A single blanket on the hay and the bed was made."

Nor was getting to Blake's diggings any fun. "The trail which we followed wound its way through a most wild and broken country," Hill noted. "We ascended hills not less than half a mile long and almost perpendicular. Up these steep and dangerous ascents we always had to walk, as it was just as much as the horses, well trained in the mountain roads, could do to carry themselves. Then we would wind down, down the steep and rugged sides of mountains steadily for half an hour, and as rapidly as was consistent with safety."

At least with Blake, Hill could say, "I never saw a happier man. . . . Mr. B. is an intelligent man of fine feelings. He is going home [to Iowa] in October." John Hitchings found the times a lot less rewarding. When the spring of 1860 opened, he and his brother-in-law washed out enough dust to pay their bills. That fall he went to South Park, where he and another ran a tunnel 200 feet under a thirty-foot gravel bed, and put in 105 sets of timbers, hoping to strike some gold where others were working out ounces a day. In December, in order to make enough to pay grocery bills, Hitchings "footed it back to Gold Hill, over 100 miles, in 5½ days and had to go to rocking frozen dirt at a spring to get provisions."

Seventy-five years later *The Denver News* wrote romantically of how the early settlers "lived off the fat of the land," but Hitchings recalled that while "the country abounded in deer, elk, antelope, rabbits, grouse, wild ducks, geese, etc.; at times, however, these were not to be had, and bread material was always expensive."

Unable to provide for the most basic necessities, discouraged men packed up wagon trains to go back to the States. The optimistic slogans they had carried west, like "Pike's Peak or Bust," "Lightning Express—Root Hog or Die," and "From Pike Co. to Pike's Peak" were changed to "Pike's Peak and Busted" as the disappointed emigrants picked their way slowly across the plains. The word "Goback" would be a term of derision for years afterward in Colorado.

Fortunately, on June 16, 1859, David Horsfal, William R. Blore, and Matthew McCaslin discovered the famous Horsfal lode about a mile east of Gold Hill. It was a rich strike, so productive that it, almost alone, kept Boulder and Gold Hill alive through the mid-1860s.

Turnips and a School

The Horsfal helped stem the returning tide of "Gobacks," but it was becoming more and more evident to many people that there had to be better ways to exist than poking a pickax blindly around a mountainside. In the fall of 1859 the Wellman brothers decided to try to serve the prospectors rather than join them. They claimed the best section of land along Boulder Creek, two and a half miles from the base of the mountains, and planted some turnips late in the season. The turnips were just starting to come up when a plague of grasshoppers arrived and destroyed the crop, but Boulder agriculture had begun.

The following spring, on May 17, the Wellmans planted a bushel and a peck of wheat that yielded forty-five bushels. The next year their wheat was "so tall that a man could tie the stalks above his head," and the yield rose to sixty bushels an acre.

Where agriculture began, irrigation followed, not only around Boulder, but throughout the semi-arid West. In June 1859, right about the time the Wellmans were beginning to think about planting their radishes, Marinus G. Smith pitched a tent near Boulder and claimed 160 acres of land. "Marine" Smith, for whom Marine Street in Boulder was named, was an interesting early-day figure whose name pops up constantly throughout the early years. In 1859 he joined William G. Pell and dug one of the first irrigation ditches around Boulder. In 1879, when lawyers attempted to settle water rights conflicts through a system of "first in time, first in right," Smith's ditch was recognized as one of the three earliest rights in the entire South Platte watershed. In 1860 the Howard and Anderson ditches were dug, and these early water rights are probably worth more today than the gold that originally brought the settlers to this area.

With agriculture and irrigation under way, there remained only one more industry to complete the backbone of Boulder's livelihood, ranching. Thanks to Anthony Arnett, it

Ranching in Boulder began in the spring of 1860 when Anthony Arnett brought a hundred heifers across the plains. (*Boulder Historical Society*)

began early in 1860. Born in Alsace-Lorraine in 1819, Arnett came to the United States when he was about nine and eventually followed the gold rush to California on a windjammer. Arnett freighted in the gold country, operated a roadhouse, and eventually followed the Pike's Peak rush to Colorado in 1859. According to one account he was once offered 160 acres of prairie land for a barrel of molasses and turned it down. The land became the heart of downtown Denver.

Impressed with the mild winter climate, Arnett decided to winter cattle around Boulder and brought a hundred heifers across the plains in the spring of 1860. By that year coal mining was under way at Marshall. Thus, within a short time, the Boulder valley saw the birth of three industries that would be critical to its existence for years to come.

Things were definitely beginning to happen around Boulder. In the fall of 1859 H.T. Graham brought out a three stamp mill (a device for crushing ore) and used the water of Left Hand Creek near Gold Hill to power it in the spring of 1860. In July Matt McCaslin and Richard Blore of the Horsfal mine went to Denver to intercept Robert and Cary Culver and persuaded them to bring their stamp mill to Gold Hill rather than take it to the Gregory District. The Culvers' stream quartz mill was the first one in Boulder County. The arrival of mills, as primitive as they were, meant a more efficient means of getting the valuable ore out of the rock. By the end of 1860 there were twenty-five mills around Gold Hill alone. Thanks to Andrew Douty and his family, who arrived in 1859, the area also had a flour mill near the iron furnace of Joseph M. Marshall, four miles from Boulder.

On July 1, 1860, a young man passed through Boulder on his way to Gold Hill and Left Hand where he was to help erect one of the quartz mills. Having been a school teacher in New York and Iowa, Abner R. Brown noticed that the groups of school-aged children playing in the streets numbered more than two to each house. Upon being told that there was no school in Boulder, Brown said that if he didn't like mining or milling he would return in two weeks and start one. Two weeks later Brown was back. Boulder was about to get the first public school in Colorado. Brown had forty pupils and received a dollar and a half per month per pupil. He hired a 12'x20' room in a log cabin for $10 a month from a man named Street, who lived in the cabin's other room with his family of five. Brown must have had a sense of humor, at least, for years later he wrote, "My room was nicely furnished for the price, as follows: The floor was painted a beautiful yellowish drab color (the virgin soil), and artistically inlaid with nodules of various sizes and colors, arising from the surface at irregular distances, some of which may have been a rare species of marble for aught I know, or some other variety of precious stones."

This was before J.W. Partridge arrived with his saw-mill and shingle machine, so the original cabin roof provided "the privilege of looking up into the blue sky or gathering clouds any time of day, or seeing the stars at night, between the shakes. But in case of wind storms [and the wind does blow in Boulder!]—whew! one could see neither sky nor clouds, nor each other inside the cabin."

Brown taught the school for three months before the citizens decided to build a good frame school building, 24'x36', with a ten-foot ceiling and a real brick chimney. Brown, a carpenter, agreed to help cut the logs as well as do the carpentry, and the citizens agreed to give him board without charge. On October 15, 1860, the school was completed at a cost of about $1200. It stood on the corner of Fifteenth and Walnut, where Central School was built in 1872.

One of the favorite old tales connected with the building of the school concerned the unwritten law that when a tree had been cut down it belonged to the person who found it if it were not used within a given time. As recounted by the *Camera* seventy-five years later, David H. Nichols cut some trees for the school one day, but when he went to gather them he found someone appropriating them. Nichols said the logs were for the school; the other cited the unwritten

Boulder's first schoolhouse, built in 1860, was the first public school in Colorado Territory. (*Colorado Historical Society*)

law. A fight broke out, and, as related in the rosy language of the old paper, "The purloiner of the timber proved to be the stronger of the two men and was getting the best of the fight when Mr. Nichols tripped the antagonist who fell flat on his back in a narrow gulley with Nichols on top."

The "purloiner" told Nichols he could have the logs, but Nichols said the terms had changed: he could get up if he helped reload the logs on Nichols' ox-cart. A bargain was made and the school had its logs.

A less often cited story, told by Mrs. Nichols, is full of the sentiment and pathos so often found in tales of the early West. According to her recollections, dictated years later, while the town was meeting to discuss how to raise money for the school, a large man sat in the back of the room dressed in high boots and corduroy with a bandana knotted around his neck.

"He was a person of few words about whom little was known," said Mrs. Nichols, "but who had gained the respect of the community. He had listened quietly and intently. He arose, addressed the chairman and as he slowly came forward took from his pocket a very much soiled and badly

mussed handkerchief a corner of which he was endeavoring
to unknot. As he reached the front of the room he turned
and faced the group saying, 'When I was about to drive away
from home my little girl came running to me and placed in
my hands this coin which she had treasured for years and
said "Daddy you may need this to buy clothing or food. Or
you may want to donate it to some worthy cause where it
may help some other child." I too have treasured it but am
giving it to you in memory of her, and I am sure it would be
her wish that you use it to help other children gain useful
knowledge now that I have no child to educate.' He then
placed a five dollar gold piece on the table by the presiding
officer and left the room. Other donations followed and by
fall Boulder had the first school house in Colorado."

The Burro Express

It must have been an exciting time for a struggling community, for that fall Boulder also got its first post office, a
sure sign of stability in any frontier settlement. The first
postmaster was a Dr. Williams, and the first government
post office was in a small, one story log house on the present
site of 1219 Pearl. Before then a post office was kept in a soap
box in one of the stores. Mail was brought in from Denver by
express and private conveyance. It cost fifty cents to bring in
a letter and a quarter to take one out to Denver, where it
would be sent by express to points on the Missouri River.
"Express" didn't always have the connotation it does today.
For several years the mail went to Denver with a man
named Rhodes who had two burros. He rode one and
packed the mail on the other, going to Denver one day and
returning the next. Around Boulder the deliveries may have
been a little faster. In 1866 Edward Viele covered his route
from Boulder to Valmont, White Rock, and Burlington
[Longmont] on horseback, carrying the mail in a couple of
saddle bags. Because the section between White Rock and
Burlington was so straight he called it the Gunbarrel Road,
giving us a name that has lasted to today.

Dr. Williams remained postmaster until July 5, 1861, when President Lincoln signed the commission for A.J. Macky, for whom Macky Auditorium at the university is named. Macky's designation as postmaster was for Boulder, Jackson County, Territory of Colorado. The name Jackson County was given by the pioneers who drafted a constitution for a Jefferson Territory in October 1859. When Congress officially created a territory on February 28, 1861, it accepted the name Jackson County. However, when the first general assembly convened, the name Boulder County was given and Boulder County became one of Colorado's original seventeen counties.

A Bill for a University

Boulder was represented in the first territorial legislature by Charles F. Holly, an early settler who also became a captain in the Second Colorado Cavalry and a judge. In the spring of 1866 Judge Holly summoned a grand jury into session and was promptly indicted with adultery. According to a newspaper account, the honorable judge had been caught in the most compromising circumstances with the wife of a physician in Central City. The suit asked $10,000 for "the theft of his wife's affections" and no less than $500,000 more "for board." Holly was removed from office but subsequently found innocent, according to a letter he wrote to the *Rocky Mountain News*. He then went to New Mexico where he made and lost a fortune.

Even without his flamboyant extra-judicial activities, Holly's name would be firmly etched in Boulder's past. When he lived in Gold Hill, Holly was known by Robert Culver, who had brought the first quartz mill to Boulder County in 1860. Culver, of New England ancestry, had an interest in higher education and began working for a university at Boulder as early as 1861. Holly wanted to represent the area in the legislature and was recognized as being an intelligent man. But if an old story is true, Culver must have been pretty quick as well.

Every mining camp was entitled to a delegate at the

convention, and the story goes that several new camps suddenly arose. Culver appeared at the convention in Golden with the proxies of all of them, became secretary of the convention, and secured the nomination of Holly as Boulder County Representative. Holly pledged to introduce a bill to have the University of Colorado at Boulder and kept his word. He introduced his bill on October 26, 1861, and it was ratified on November 7 by Governor Gilpin. There was thus another seed planted that would come to fruition years later and be of critical significance to Boulder's future.

It would be fifteen years before the Territory of Colorado became the State of Colorado, but by 1861 Boulder County had finally received its name. Over four centuries the land had been claimed by Spain, France, and the United States. Within two years Boulder had been part of "St. Vrain's County, Territory of Nebraska," "Jackson County, Territory of Jefferson," and now "Boulder County, Territory of Colorado."

Throughout all this time the Arapahoes had assumed the land was theirs. It always had been and the U.S. government had said it was. But time was closing in on the ancestral homes of the Indians. The West was destined to become an enormous setting for the inevitable clash of two cultures. It took most of the century for the entire drama to unfold, but for Boulder and the rest of the plains, the critical year was to be 1864.

Sand Creek

In keeping with the pattern that had emerged from the time of the early mountain men, there weren't many problems with the Indians when the settlers first arrived. Alp Wright, who had a claim near the mouth of the canyon, said the Arapahoes were "numerous, armed, and saucy" early in 1859, but he seemed most annoyed at "their habit of standing around while his party was frying bacon, and, with the worm in the end of their ramrods, hooking slices from the frying pan." Old Man Baker was shot on Gold Hill by an Indian, supposedly a passing Ute, and there was a raid on stock and cattle in June of '63, recalled John Hitchings, "but that was the amount of their deviltry in all this section."

David G. Taylor, who came to Boulder in June 1860, felt there was more danger from whites than from Indians in the valley, referring to the "Regulators" and the "Vigilantes." "The Regulators were organized for the purpose of protecting themselves, while the vigilantes organized to protect themselves against the Regulators, who were a desperate band. Every man in the county went armed."

Certainly all seemed awed by the great Arapahoe antelope hunt in the fall of 1860 when 400 riders surrounded a herd of thousands, chasing the antelope round and round with relays of ponies until the antelope lay down and were slaughtered for winter meat in a hollow near Valmont.

This was the last such harvest in the valley, but the Indians were becoming both a nuisance and a threat. They knew that a civil war had broken out among the whites and that many of the troops had been transferred back east to fight the war. But they also knew that wagons were still heading west, and with the arrival of more and more settlers, the frequency of attacks on wagon trains and homesteads began to increase. By 1863 and 1864 the plains had become so dangerous that mail from the East was being brought in by way of Panama and San Francisco, requiring seven to ten weeks for delivery.

Rumor spread around Boulder that the George Andrews party had been attacked recrossing the plains and murdered to a man. Then word came back than an emigrant train with women and children had been massacred. The Andrews party eventually returned to Boulder with a train of supplies, delayed but unharmed, but by then Boulder was living in fear. Governor Evans called for "100 day volunteers" to defend the Territory, and Boulder began digging trenches along Twelfth and Thirteenth streets for defense. Fort Chambers, an adobe structure on the G. W. Chambers farm below Valmont, was built and families prepared to gather there if need be.

At one point attack seemed imminent and the settlers

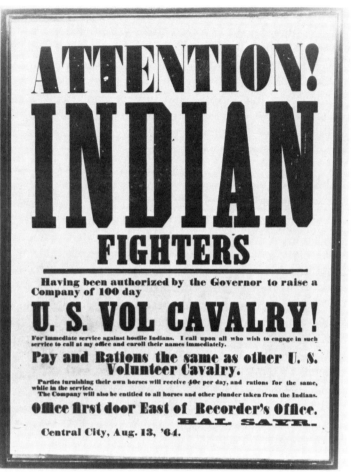

ATTENTION!
INDIAN
FIGHTERS

Having been authorized by the Governor to raise a Company of 100 day

U. S. VOL CAVALRY!

For immediate service against hostile Indians. I call upon all who wish to engage in such service to call at my office and enroll their names immediately.

Pay and Rations the same as other U. S. Volunteer Cavalry.

Parties furnishing their own horses will receive 40c per day, and rations for the same, while in the service.
The Company will also be entitled to all horses and other plunder taken from the Indians.

Office first door East of Recorder's Office.

HAL. SAYR.

Central City, Aug. 13, '64.

(Colorado Historical Society)

decided to abandon Boulder. At dusk a wagon train left for Denver to wait out hostilities, but by day-break, having stopped to talk frequently with outriders, they were only halfway. The light of day restored their courage and they decided to go back home.

Fort Chambers became the training headquarters for recruits, and Captain David H. Nichols was commissioned to recruit a company of one hundred men to open and defend the Platte River wagon road all the way to Julesburg. The company left Fort Chambers on September 16, 1864, and met Captain C.M. Tyler's company from Black Hawk at Valley Station, fifty miles from Julesburg. On October 9, Nichols and twenty-two men attacked the party of Big Wolf at Buffalo Springs, killing eleven, and discovering finely wrought clothing, scalps, and boxes of goods taken from wagon trains. From there Nichols moved south through the sandhills to join Colonel John Chivington on the Arkansas River. On the morning of November 29, the Boulder Company was part of the combined First and Third Regiments of Cavalry that swept down through the sand hills and attacked the waking Indians at Sand Creek.

We need not repeat or reassess the atrocities that followed. By late afternoon about 148 Southern Arapahoe and Cheyenne Indians lay dead. Men, women and children had been murdered in cold blood, scalped, and horribly mutilated in the frenzy of the attack. Among the dead were nine Cheyenne chiefs who had worked for peace. We do not know with absolute certainty, but it appears that Left Hand, the articulate, peace-seeking chief of the Arapahoes, died there as well. The attacking whites numbered between 600 and 1000 men; accounts differ. Of the 148 Indians, about two-thirds were women and children; many of the men were well beyond their fighting years. Chivington's troops had about thirteen dead and thirty-eight wounded. Two of the dead, Robert McFarland and Henry Foster, were from Boulder.

Chivington and Nichols returned to a hero's welcome in Denver and Boulder, but when congressional and military investigations followed in 1865, Chivington and Governor Evans were asked to resign their posts and did.

In 1886 historian Hubert H. Bancroft interviewed many of the early settlers in Boulder, and a great many commented that the Sand Creek massacre was a necessity and that the Indian problem had to be settled once and for all, one way or another.

Perspectives of history change with time. Rights and wrongs are relative, not absolute. To be sure, the actions at

Sand Creek were favorably viewed by many men in the region for many years. But one thing Sand Creek did not achieve was the end of the Indian question. In January 1865, in retaliation for Sand Creek, Indians severed the Platte River wagon road once again, and Colonel Thomas Moonlight proclaimed martial law in Boulder, ordering the stores and business suspended until Boulder raised another volunteer company that would help reopen the road. The war between the Plains Indians and the United States would last another twenty-five years, although few battles were to be fought in Colorado. In a sense, the interviewed settlers were right, for the Arapahoes never returned to their ancestral home in Colorado. But in a larger sense the battle at Sand Creek opened a war that wouldn't end until 1890 and the Battle of Wounded Knee.

Determination

What is perhaps most amazing about this era is that despite the occasional threat of Indian attack and the constant difficulty of simply surviving, the settlers continued to build their town. Like every other settler who dared to cross the plains, the Boulder pioneer was a resourceful, independent person who was unafraid to try his or her luck on something new.

William A. Davidson, for whom Davidson Mesa is named, first crossed the plains to California in 1850, setting out with six horses and $50. When he arrived he had fourteen horses and $1500. He made his money by ferrying passengers across the Green River. The resourceful Davidson subsequently brought a fifty stamp mill across the plains with 450 yoke of oxen, one of the largest trains ever to make the crossing. James A. Walker arrived in Boulder with $12 and made over $15,000 in ten years in the cattle business, acquiring 800 acres on a ranch seven and a half miles south of Boulder on South Boulder Slope. George R. Williamson came with one yoke of cattle and a wagon in the fall of 1858 and had a hard time making a living for years, but his perseverance paid off when he discovered the Yellow Pine mine in 1870. Williamson took out $200,000 from the mine by 1886 and turned down an offer of $750,000 for it.

The women were just as brave. In 1864, during the height of Indian troubles on the plains, the wife of Anthony Arnett set out from Illinois to join her husband in Boulder. With her were her two sons, Willamette, eighteen, and Emmett, age three. Mrs. Arnett left Fort Kearney, unaware of regulations requiring wagons to join together under armed escort for travel across the plains. Two days later they met a scout carrying dispatches for Fort Kearney, who told the Arnetts of the dangers. They were so far along he told them they might as well continue but warned them to stop for nothing along the way.

Farther along the Arnetts reached the remains of a wagon that had been attacked by Indians. A woman and her scalped husband lay alongside the trail. Here and there were the bodies of the children. The baby lay where it had been dropped after its head had been smashed against a wagon wheel.

Later the Arnetts came upon half a dozen Indian women, who shrieked at them and waved their arms. Remembering the scout's warning, Mrs. Arnett hollered, "Drive right through them, Will!" The women kicked dust in the horses faces, trying to cause a stampede, but the Arnett rigs drove through them, eventually reaching Denver to the disbelief of officials there.

But of all the people who came to Boulder, none were more dedicated and determined than the ministers and priests, who brought religion to the valley. Boulder's first preacher arrived as early as August 1859. According to his letter written in 1904 to Rev. John A. Davis of Boulder, Rev. J. Adriance gave the first religious services in Boulder on Sunday, August 14, "in the house of a Mr. Moore, at 10:30, Text John 3-6." He dined with a Mr. Williams, then "Preached at 4 P.M. from Matt. 13-23. About 50 present, and seemed to be interested. A Mr. Mitchell joined the church."

The dedicated Rev. Adriance held services in the second story of a saloon, slept on the ground with a stone for his pillow ("I could find *sweet sleep* anywhere if I could straighten out and keep warm"), and made his rounds on foot when he lost his pony. On one weekend he walked from Golden City to Boulder, preached at 10:30, and walked to Gold Hill for a service in the evening. Three days later he was back in Golden, his rounds completed. Nor was it any easier being a pastor's wife, who "of course . . . must visit on the circuit . . . . (A)s the age of buggies had not dawned in that region, and 'Prairie Schooners' were a little cumbersome, a borrowed sidesaddle met the exigencies of the case." Eight hours later, the dutiful Mrs. Adriance arrived at brother Goss's "somewhat fatigued" by her long ride.

A Sign of Stability

Thanks to Rev. Adriance, the claim to having Boulder's first church services went to the Methodists, but on July 17, 1864, the Congregationalists organized in a cottonwood grove near Valmont and went on to build Boulder's first church.

The founding force was Rev. William Crawford, a representative of the American Home Missionary Society who had come to Colorado in 1863 and founded a church at Golden. Rev. Williams acted as supply pastor for the fourteen charter members until a full time minister could be found.

Occasionally Rev. Norman McLeod of Denver, another Society representative, would preach to the congregation. On October 20, 1864, he described a strangely prophetic vision concerning Boulder in a letter written from Denver: "When I took the last look at Boulder, some weeks ago, from the mountains beyond, I saw in the future a College there, crowded with young people." But Rev. McLeod was more a practical man than a visionary, for he continued. "You can see at once the influence such an educational Institute would have on our church. It would virtually concentrate the influence of the whole neighborhood and give it a start—it would help make a congregation. . . . I shall spend 10 days going from house to house all through the country agitating the question and urging the people to act."

Thus, for the agitating Rev. McLeod, a college was a political tool, a means by which a church could grow. But his dream was not to be realized; ironically it would be the church itself that became the political factor in the imminent development of the valley.

As hard for us as it may be to believe today, there was great speculation in 1865 as to whether the county seat would wind up in Boulder, Burlington (Longmont), or Valmont. In the fall of 1865 Rev. Nathan Thompson rode 652 miles across the plains in a stage to become the first full time minister of the Congregational Church. "Would it [the county seat] stay in Boulder?" he recalled. "Burlington said no. New born Valmont said no. Even primeval Boulder hardly dared to say yes." In words that sound hauntingly applicable to the protracted Boulder-Louisville shopping center dispute 115 years later, Rev. Thompson added, "The future business center of the valley was the great question."

After much debate the church leaders decided in favor of Boulder, and on the third Sunday in February 1866 church services were held in Boulder's school house on the corner of Fifteenth and Walnut. It was a daring decision, for at that time not one member of the congregation lived in Boulder. All were at least four or five miles away and would have to go to church in farm wagons or prairie schooners over rough roads, fording a creek along the way. But if a church were to grow, it had to go where it could attract new members.

Boulder of course was delighted. The arrival of the church meant one more sign of stability and respectability for a struggling town. When the schoolhouse became inadequate and Rev. Thompson wanted to build a permanent church building, Boulder's founding fathers were more than ready to lend a helping hand. Jonathan Tourtellot and Frederick Squires, who were not Congregationalists, gave Rev. Thompson $300 to help get the church started. Anthony Arnett, Charles Dabney, Alpheus Wright, Clinton Tyler, and Granville Berkley, also non-Congregationalists, chipped in as well, and these were times when there wasn't much cash around. Boulder's leaders lent a personal hand too. Marinus Smith hauled sand from the creek for the masons, A.J. Macky supplied timber and joists. Legislator Thomas Graham helped lay the floor.

With the help of Fred Squires, the miners raised money for a bell. "Little Thompson has the church about done," he would tell them. "You will want to hear it when you come down. There are so many of you we want only a little from each. Just a dollar, that's all, although some of you would like to give more."

In 1869 a thousand-pound bell was hauled out by ox-team and unloaded at the base of the tower. In July 1870, Boulder's Congregational Church was dedicated free of debt. It stood on the present site of 1125 Pine Street, serving its members for nearly forty years until torn down in 1905 to make way for a new church building. The original bell is mounted on a stone base in front of the new church, along with a plaque placed there by the Arapahoe Chapter of the Daughters of the American Revolution.

Dark Stains on the Pioneers

Having looked to Valmont for a church, why not a newspaper? "Ambitious little Valmont . . . usually called Bugtown, on account of the monstrous size and fierce vigor of the bed bugs they grew down there" not only had one, but the *Boulder Valley News* was the only newspaper in all of Colorado north of Denver, according to Joseph Wolff, who arrived in 1861 and wrote a series of articles for the *Daily Camera* forty-seven years later.

A newspaper, wrote Wolff, "was the best asset any town could have at that time, and the people of Boulder were ready to go to any length to keep it." Bugtown, Boulder's "fierce rival," had managed to sneak in a printing press and had a man named Scouten to set the type and edit. "Scout," as he was called, spent a lot of his free time in Boulder

The *Boulder News* (1889-1914) was one of many early Boulder newspapers. There are no known copies of Boulder's first newspaper, the *Boulder Valley News*, which Boulder allegedly "acquired" from "ambitious little Valmont." (*Boulder Historical Society*)

where there was a "genial set, besides two saloons" that kept a fine supply of Taos Lightning.

"Scout liked it, the Lightning," Wolff mused. "He liked any old thing in the shape of liquor. The generosity of our saloon loafers appealed strongly to 'Scout'. It kept him always supplied, and most of the time drunk. This generosity had an element of selfishness in it, for it was intended to get him deeply in love with the town, so that we could steal the paper away from Bugtown. That, it must be admitted, was a dark stain on the reputation of the pioneers. But they wanted a newspaper and the cheapest way was to steal it. So while 'Scout' was gloriously drunk, they took a wagon, went down to Bugtown and loaded the concern onto the wagon. They triumphantly came into town with a whole printing office on the one wagon. When Scout got sober he found himself slightly upside down. But he took the change like a philosopher, and promptly issued the first newspaper the town of Boulder ever had." The *Boulder Valley News*, a weekly, ran in Boulder from April 3, 1867, to September 1868. No copies are known to exist.

The acquisition of the newspaper wasn't to be the only "dark stain on the reputation of the pioneers." On June 29, 1867, the *Rocky Mountain News* reported a hanging in Boulder. According to the story, a man named William Tull stole some horses from James Tourtellot. Robert Culver and Henry Green set out in pursuit and tracked Tull to an Indian camp on the Cache la Poudre where he had an Indian wife. Tull surrendered quietly when the party surrounded him and was taken back to town and turned over to Deputy Sheriff Anderson. On the way back Tull allegedly confessed to other thefts as well as having escaped from the Denver jail the preceding winter.

The party returned on a Sunday morning. On Monday Tull's body was found hanging from a tree across the bridge at the foot of Pearl Street. Deputy Anderson subsequently testified to a coroner's jury, "I had the said man in my charge; he was under arrest for larceny. On the night of the twenty-third of June, between twelve and one o'clock, there were five men, unknown to me, who rushed into the room and demanded the prisoner and told me if I made any resistance I was a dead man; there were more men outside of the room; they went to the prisoner and told him he had stayed with the sheriff long enough, and to get up and put on his clothes and go along with them, for they would take care of him. They then pulled him out of bed, and demanded of me the key to the handcuffs and told me they wanted to take the handcuffs off: I gave the key to one of the men. They then took him off, as I suppose, across the bridge over Boulder Creek, and at the same time leaving some of the men holding my door."

Tull was about twenty-six, well-educated, moved in good society, and came from Ohio. Joseph Wolff remembered a few other details in 1908. The deputy had a sleeping room over the blacksmith shop on Twelfth and Pearl that was reached by an outside stairway only three feet wide. At the top was a small platform that could not accomodate three standing men. The stairway and platform were within less than two feet of the residence of Anthony Arnett, which was occupied by his family at the time. It was in this room that Anderson had Tull in irons.

When Tull heard the mob coming he "begged the deputy to take off his irons and let him have a revolver so that he might defend himself," wrote Wolff. "But neither of these requests were granted. A single man, with the courage of a louse, standing on that platform, could have defended the prisoner with a club. So few of them, and so quiet were they, that there was no noise made to awake the family of Mr. Arnett. . . ." The mob took Tull to a tree "so low that they could not find a limb high enough to keep Tull's feet from touching the ground. Here they literally strangled their victim to death. The noise of his strangling was heard a distance of several blocks, though the people did not know what caused it."

Wolff called the inquest "the most contemptible legal farce that ever disgraced any community. The whole affair was utterly brutal, and it certainly looked like collusion between the peace officers and the mob. In fact, if there were no other evidence of this, it could be found in the inhuman remark, made in Tull's presence at the hotel, by the sheriff and before he had been delivered over to the deputy to be surrendered to the mob, 'This affair will not cost the county anything'. . . . (T)o the eternal disgrace of the city of Boulder, this unmitigated outrage was organized by a few men who thus showed themselves to be much greater criminals than their victim."

The Tull affair was lamentable, but what followed was extraordinary. On May 15, 1874, the *County News* reported that Judge Belford and another man were walking along the road near the cottonwood tree where Tull had been lynched, "when at the same moment they both discovered what appeared to be the form of a man hanging to a tree. Both stopped still in astonishment and then started towards the tree, when the form seemed to slowly walk away backwards, carrying the rope in its hands, by which a moment before it hung. It motioned to its mouth, as though wanting to speak, but unable. Slowly it faded away out of sight, leaving the two gentlemen who saw it wondering whether their eyes were deceived. Though they waited long, it did not come again."

The story also reported that a similar experience happened to Constable R. L. Long, while returning from a business trip one evening, frightening his horse as well. The form was hanging in the tree, then came toward Long, motioning to its mouth as if in great pain, and wildly pointing towards the east, as if it wanted him to go there with it. But when he rode near, it vanished. Yet a third person, a Dr. Lane, had a similar experience, prompting the *News* to conclude:

> That it is something beyond human comprehension, if not something supernatural, will not for a moment be denied. That it is the ghost of the man who was hung to the trees years ago, we are not ready to admit, for we have never believed much in spirits, other than liquid. But that it may be the spirit of the dead thief, come back to point out its executioners, or to reveal some secret that is darkly hidden, can not be denied, for when men of the standing and respectability of the gentlemen who have seen this apparition, solemnly aver that they were not deceived, we must believe that there is something in the story.

This story, perhaps the best documented of Boulder's ghost stories, is not the only one. Tom Horn, one of the last paid gunfighters of the old west, was buried in Boulder's Columbia Cemetery by a sister who lived here, and his ghost has allegedly been seen moving restlessly among the stones. In 1977 the *Boulder Daily Camera* carried a story about a family in Left Hand Canyon that has been physically dragged about by "wispy visitors." Commenting on the community's general disbelief in such things, Robert Cook, owner of a Boulder home with a more unobtrusive spirit, called Boulder a very practical, very middle class town without much sense of humor.

The comment brings to mind the observation of Nathaniel Hill in 1864 that "Boulder City is the most Yankee of any settlement I have seen in Colorado." Since Hill was staying with Jonathan A. Tourtellot, who had come from Rhode Island, and was out to visit the mines of Henry Blake, a graduate of an Ohio college, perhaps he was referring to the number of pioneers who had come out to Boulder from New England and the northern states. But he might just as well have been thinking of the straight-laced, rugged individualism, self reliance, and dogged, almost Puritanic determination of the people who were committed to building the town. True, there were those for whom the presence of two saloons could taint a city. And no one was claiming that Boulder itself—one schoolhouse, two hotels, a general store, carpenter shop, blacksmith shop, doctor's office, county clerk's office, and two saloons, all made of logs or boards—was a thing of beauty.

A Spot Sacred To Beauty

Poor Tull may have been lynched; Boulder may have stolen the newspaper from archrival Valmont. But those dark stains were more than balanced by such men as Rev. Thompson and Abner Brown, who would stay long enough to build a church and a school. Drawn by the prospects in the mines or for farming the valley's fertile lands, people kept finding their way to Boulder, and let there be no doubt that even then people were struck by the view of Boulder when they reached the top of the hills to the east.

The reaction of Rev. Thompson would be echoed by countless thousands who followed his arrival in October 1865: "The sun was westering, yet well above the mountains. Only a few fleecy clouds were in the sky. The air was of that clearness, indescribable but such as every Coloradoan knows. Each dwelling in the little town, 5 or 6 miles away, every building on the few ranches that had been appropriated along the two creeks, every stack, every rick, even the stock, feeding on the open prairie, seemed distinct and almost near enough for each to be individually identified. The prospect from that bluff, overlooking the place of my first Christian service after leaving the schools was so attractive as to make me feel very hopeful and therefore very happy."

Rev. Thompson was such an optimist he could even be

positive about Boulder's horrendous winds. Writing to the *Boulder County News* from Massachusetts in 1879, he reflected, "Well, there was some economy in those winds. For then our kerosene cost us four dollars a gallon—now I get it for ten cents—and we all would have a light unless nature forcibly forbade."

Thompson was hardly alone in singing the praises of Boulder. In 1869 he was joined most enthusiastically by Samuel Bowles, Editor of the *Springfield* (Massachusetts) *Republican*. Bowles, one of the most ardent fans of the West, had a special warmth toward Colorado and loved to write about its great mountains and parks, its abundant flora and fauna, and wonderful air. In *Our New West*, Bowles described his arrival in Boulder, tired and hungry after a long day in the mountains that had seen his party through brilliant sunshine and a sudden late summer, high-country snow storm. ". . . following the south Boulder Creek, came at last, wet and weary, into the nearly deserted mining village of South Boulder. Here we found welcome around the fire at the post office; a deserted cabin was thrown open to us for our baggage and our meals; and a big barn's loft with fresh hay furnished a magnificent bedroom. We dried, we ate, having fresh meat, cream, and vegetables added to our bill, and we slept, all in luxury. . . ."

Thinking of his preceding day on South Boulder Creek, Bowles recalled "the greenest of grass, the bluest of harebells, the reddest of painter's brush, the yellowest of sunflowers and buttercups, [a]ll with the brightest of sun and bluest of sky," and concluded "that no spot in all our travel is more sacred to beauty than this of our noon camp on Boulder." In his guide to *The Pacific Railroad*, also written in 1869, Bowles mentioned a ride up through the mountains by Boulder Creek as one of the suggestions for the cross country traveler who wanted to leave the transcontinental railroad at Cheyenne to see some of Colorado.

Actually, by 1869 Boulder was making a real effort to look like a civilized little town. A reading room was established and clubs were formed for literature, music and baseball.

Boulder Canyon; drawing by Thomas Moran. (From *Picturesque America, Vol. II, 1874*)

You could read the local newspaper and find an ad for a piano. Or you could follow the efforts of blacksmith Peter Jasper to build a "three-wheeled velocipede." Eighteen sixty-nine was also the year a hundred local women gave $93.50 to the editor of the newspaper when he refused to advertise for liquor sellers, foreshadowing the days of the temperance movement a decade later.

A Toll-Collecting Magpie and Good Ham and Eggs

Eighteen sixty-nine also brought the following ad in the February 17 edition of the *Boulder County Pioneer*: "Wells-Fargo & Co. have offered to put stage coaches on the road from Cheyenne to Boulder and on to Black Hawk if Boulder would build a road into the mountains."

The importance of good roads as a means to attract people had been obvious from the earliest days of '59. Mrs. Nichols remembered the outriders who met them in eastern Colorado and tried to persuade the Nicholses to go to Denver rather than Boulder. If a person didn't have a particular place in mind, a simple thing like a decent road could help with the decision.

Hoping to turn the traffic toward Boulder and make it the mining center of the region, Henry C. Norton built a toll bridge across the Platte River at old Fort St. Vrain and intended to build a road on to the Gregory mines at Black Hawk. The settlers gave all they could, but ultimately the project turned out to be too great for their means.

In 1859-60 a large townsite was laid out at the mouth of Left Hand Canyon for a place to be called Altona. The St. Vrain, Altona, Gold Hill and Gregory Road Company built a road from Altona to Aikens Gulch on Left Hand Creek, then up to Gold Hill, but the road failed and Altona became a paper city. In 1861-62 Norton and George Williamson built a road up Bear Canyon to Black Hawk and Central City, but it was washed out after a cloudburst. Four more attempts at Bear Canyon would be washed away by 1885.

Gordon and McHenry managed to build a road up Sunshine Canyon that joined Four Mile Creek, turned right at Orodell (junction of Four Mile and Boulder canyons), and went up to Sugar Loaf and on to the north of Caribou. This was supposed to be a military road over Arapaho Pass into Middle Park, but it never got that far.

Boulder Canyon was impassable. The cliffs came right down to the stream, and, since a man couldn't make his way on foot, there was a lot of early dispute over whether a wagon road could ever be constructed through it. On March 11, 1864, the Territorial Legislature granted a charter for a Boulder Valley and Central City wagon road. A company was organized with a capital stock of $50,000, and Boulder's leading men joined in: the Wellmans, Anthony Arnett, Tourtellot and Squires, J.P. Maxwell and C.M. Tyler subscribed $10,000. Charles Dabney and Daniel Pound were among the others who joined.

Construction began in March 1865 under Maxwell's supervision. Three months later the road had cost $9000 and reached Four Mile Creek. It took until the following year, but the road pushed on to Magnolia Hill, South Boulder Creek, the Enterprise Road (between Golden Gate and Black Hawk—the main toll road from Denver) and on to Black Hawk. Suddenly, Boulder was connected with the mines at Black Hawk and Central City. Toll gates were set up at the mouth of Boulder Canyon and the foot of Magnolia Hill, and many an oldtimer came to remember Mrs. Norton's magpie that sat on the canyon gate and cried, "Pay your toll! Pay your toll!" Charges were $1 for wagon and team, or two horses, mules or oxen; 25¢ for each additional animal; loose animals 10¢ a head. Parties passing over toll roads for religious services or attending funerals passed free of charge.

When the Wells Fargo ad came along, trade worth hundreds of dollars a day was pouring into Central City. While the road over Magnolia already existed, Boulder would likely attract more of that trade with a more direct route. Arnett, Widner and Pound formed another company

Tollhouse at the mouth of Boulder Canyon. Farther up were thirty-three bridges, a toll-collecting magpie, and good ham and eggs. (*Boulder Historical Society*)

and surveyed a route up Boulder Canyon from the foot of Magnolia Hill through the Narrows to Brown's Ranch (Nederland). The walls were so steep that they had to wait until the stream was frozen in winter in order to survey, but they found the route to Black Hawk would be a full six miles shorter.

If there were any doubt that the difficult road would be worth completing, it disappeared when a rich silver strike was made at Caribou in the fall of 1869. The roadbuilders crossed and re-crossed the stream, avoiding the never ending cliffs. By the time they finished in 1871, there were thirty-three bridges in the canyon between Nederland and Boulder. The road had cost the men $10,000 each. Lee and Walter Smith built a stage station called the American House at the head of the Narrows, where stage drivers changed horses and Hank Pryor became known for his good ham and eggs. A toll gate was placed in the canyon, but the investors never came close to seeing their investment returned. Upkeep was far too great. Many sections were "corduroy," made of poles and boulders with round logs for the bed, and remained that way for years. As late as 1913 the

Caribou. After the rich silver strike of 1869, a town arose from nothing. By 1880 it had its own newspaper and a population of 549. (*Boulder Historical Society*)

Boulder Canyon road was known as narrow, steep, and tortuous. Even today, although vastly improved, it remains one of the most dangerous roads in the state.

Wells Fargo never produced their stages, but thanks to the newly completed road, which went on to the mines at Caribou, Boulder began to enjoy a trade worth several thousand dollars a month.

What the Horsfal lode had meant to the '60s, the Caribou was to the '70s and beyond. In fact, the strike proved to be one of the great mining events in Boulder County. The lode was discovered by William J. Martin, Samuel Mishler, George Lytle, Hugh McCammon, Samuel Conger, and John Rickel. According to a paper presented by Prof. Percy S. Fritz in 1945, the claim was named by Lytle after the Caribou district of British Columbia, where he had once mined.

The Caribou was the first patented mining claim in Boulder County and one of the first in the state. Its main shaft was 520' deep, and by 1876 a pamphlet on The Grand Island

Caribou's mines kept Boulder alive through the 1870s and beyond. Today very little remains. (*Boulder Historical Society*)

Mining District proudly claimed that "3250 square fathoms have been broken, producing somewhat over $754,000 in silver or a realized value of $230 per fathom, which is, for instance, twice as much as the average value per fathom of the valuable copper mines on Lake Superior . . . and three times as much as the average paying mines in Cornwall, England as the Cambria, Dolcoath, and others."

The Caribou eventually produced $20 million worth of silver, some of which paved Grant's pathway into the Teller House at Central City. Widely publicized, it attracted new people and new money to the region. The town of Caribou arose, which had its own newspaper and a population of 549, according to the 1880 census.

Then, on May 1, 1872, Christian Holk and Joseph Steppler located the Red Cloud, with its rare telluride of gold and silver, in the Gold Hill district. When a six ton batch yielded $400 per ton, a new rush was on at Gold Hill. Shortly after, a richer telluride discovery was made at the American mine, and Sunshine was born. The mountains were booming again, and so, at last, was Boulder.

PART II
"A Hideous Collection of Houses"

A Curious Deed and a Mile of Mud

Prosperity hardly arrived overnight. In 1870 Boulder's population was still only 343. George Crofutt's 1872 *Transcontinental Tourist's Guide* couldn't even give space to Boulder, although it had ample room for Golden ("This 'Lowell' of Colorado"), Black Hawk, and even Evans, the Weld County seat.

By 1873 Boulder still had no water mains. Housewives took water from the creek or the irrigation ditches. The sidewalks were raised wooden planks, and the town square was fenced with chains so men could tie up their oxen, horses, and mules while trading. Isabella Bird, the adventurous Englishwoman who traveled through the area on horseback that year, called Boulder a "hideous collection of frame houses on the burning plain." Even Timothy William Stanton, an 1883 University of Colorado graduate who went on to become a leading figure in American geology, had to admit that the beauty of Boulder was "more in the surroundings than in the town itself," when he arrived as a child in 1874.

But during these years Boulder was taking significant steps toward becoming more than a hideous collection of houses. Boulder businessmen decided to bring the railroad to town in 1870 and tried to extend the Denver & Boulder Valley line from Erie to Boulder. An unlikely 420-420 tie vote destroyed the measure that fall, but Boulder citizens said they would grade and tie the line if the railroad would lay the iron. The railroad agreed and a great groundbreaking ceremony followed in March 1871.

Boulder kept its part of the bargain, but the railroad didn't finish laying the track until September 1873. By then the

Well into the 1870s, Boulder's muddy streets inspired epithets, some poetic. Photograph was taken from Lovers' (Sunset) Hill, looking down Fourteenth Street. (*Boulder Historical Society*)

long awaited arrival of the Denver & Boulder Valley was anti-climactic: the Colorado Central had been there for months. Nevertheless, Boulder was now connected by rail with the rest of the world.

The new road up Boulder Canyon, which even Isabella Bird had called "superb," was bringing more and more freight wagons into town from Caribou, Central City, and Gold Hill. Streets needed repair and dogs were running around. Fire protection was a growing concern, and so was a municipal water supply. And oh the mud! One irate, but poetic citizen complained to the newspaper of

> The mud, the miserable mud
> Into its depths you go with a thud
> That causes the sticky nasty clay
> To slide up your boots in a horrible way. . . .

Boulder City was growing up. Having called itself a city for over a decade, now it had to start acting like one. Anthony Arnett, James P. Maxwell, Marinus Smith, Frederick Squires, and Alpheus Wright were asked to serve as city fathers and to elect officers and set a time for meetings. On

November 4, 1871, Boulder was officially incorporated under county authority and held its first elections the following April. Twelfth Street (Broadway) was graded and board sidewalks appeared. Boulder acquired a "calaboose" and fire-fighting companies were organized. Above all, law and order prevailed.

On the day of incorporation, the town trustees appointed Oscar Allen as constable and subsequently charged him with a broad range of peace keeping duties. Nudity, gambling, rioting, prostitution, and intoxication were outlawed, along with riding or driving a horse "inordinately" and firing a cannon, gun, or "squib-cracker" without permission. Profane language could draw a fine of up to $500. By the end of 1871 Constable Allen had made many arrests, and by the spring of 1873 the *News* could observe that "business in the courts is remarkably dull." Boulder had come a long way from the early days of "club rule" and punishments meted out by the local vigilance committee. Another sign of the old frontier had begun to slip away.

Boulder's incorporation included the original townsite and three additional parcels of land. According to one venerable source, Boulder, while about to plunge strongly into the future, also had a most unusual tie to the past.

H.C. Hickman came to Boulder for his health in 1922. He lived here for sixty years until he died late in 1982 at the age of ninety-five. Shortly after his arrival, Hickman became owner of the Boulder County Abstract Company, which had been founded by A.E. Lea in 1871. According to a story told by Hickman years ago, Lea filed the deed to the property of the original townsite. The deed was signed by President Ulysses S. Grant. Its original owner was a Revolutionary War widow who had probably never even heard of Boulder.

According to Hickman's story, in 1855 the federal government decided to reward soldiers who had fought in the Revolution, or their widows, with gifts of free land. One of these soldiers was Joseph Weston of Maine, who later married a woman named Sarah.

Weston died in 1838, but when the federal government passed the act, Sarah, in her 90s, filed her claim and received Bonus Certificate No. 36.557. The 160 acres under this claim was to become the town of Boulder.

No one knows how this deed passed from Sarah Weston to Peter Housel, later the probate judge of Boulder County. Hickman's research suggests that Mrs. Weston might have sold the certificate to a land speculator, or, some New Englander may have dealt with Mrs. Weston before heading west. Mrs. Weston was from Cannan, Maine, and records show that three sons of the Parlin family went west from there. A David Parlin was probate judge for Boulder County just before Peter Housel. Another possibility concerns the historian Amos Bixby, who came to Boulder with his brother in 1862. Bixby was a relative of the Westons.

Whatever happened, Mrs. Weston disposed of her deed in 1856, and it turned up with the document that transferred the holdings to Peter Housel. It was signed September 11, 1869, by President Grant "in trust for the several use and benefit of occupants of Boulder Townsite according to their respective interests under the Townsite Act of Congress approved May 23, 1844." Given Sarah Weston's age at the time, Boulder's first owner probably never saw the land she owned and most likely never heard of "Boulder" or even "Colorado" which didn't even exist at the time of her acquisition and transfer.

The deed described the townsite as a square that included "the area from Hill [Mapleton Avenue] to Valley [Arapahoe Avenue]." To the west, the border was between 10th and 11th Streets, and to the east, between 17th and 18th Streets. But with Boulder booming and the railroad in town, Boulder developers and promoters laid out seventeen new additions between 1870 and 1878, when Boulder was incorporated under the statutes of the new State of Colorado.

By then, according to one impressed woman from Massachusetts, the houses were "so universally of brick that one might style it a 'brick city.' " Boulder had become a land of plenty: "Gardens are universal, and the family which cannot show its large watermelons, immense squashes, the sweetest of corn, cucumbers, beans, etc., etc., can depend upon its neighbors for such." It would take a few more years, but by 1892 a man from Worcester came to Boulder and said, "Boulder is essentially a city of beautiful homes."

Boulder no longer had to call itself "Boulder City," trying to sound like something it wasn't. Boulder was a city, by 1882 a city of the second class, no less (based upon population). From now on, simply "Boulder" would do.

A place whose county mineral production increased from $250,000 a year to twice that within three years was ready for a bank. In 1871 George Corning opened up his Bank of

West Boulder, 1870. "A hideous collection of houses" according to one traveler, but during the decade Boulder's population would rise from 343 to over 3000. (*Boulder Historical Society*)

Boulder. In 1874 Charles and Walter Buckingham opened up a private bank, which they decided to call the National State Bank in 1877. In 1939 the *Boulder Daily Camera* saluted "the longest-lived institution in the city." Charles G. Buckingham, then 92, was in his 65th year with the bank, "a record not approached by any other banker in America," and the bank could proudly claim that "in the long history of the bank, no depositor has ever lost a penny." Given that the bank had weathered the panics of 1893, 1907, and 1929, it was quite a claim to make.

Buckingham became a prominent citizen of Boulder, contributing to various causes throughout his life. In 1922 he bought the land surrounding Boulder Falls when a mining operation threatened to desecrate the site. In 1877 he gave $2000 to found a library at the university.

The university. The idea had lain dormant since the bill for establishing a university at Boulder had been passed in 1861. In 1880 Amos Bixby said, "The founders understood that it would bring here the best class of citizens, the intellectual, the cultured, the moral, coming both for the education of their children and for the sake of the society that clusters about prosperous seats of learning."

The early settlers also undoubtedly realized that a university represented a permanent asset to the community. The mountains could go boom or bust, but a university was an important constant.

Other towns realized this as well, and in 1874 the territorial legislature battled once again over where the university ought to be. According to one tale it was thanks again to Anthony Arnett that Boulder became the site. John Topping, a member of the legislature from southern Colorado, had crossed the plains with Arnett years before and was staying with the Arnetts in Boulder before the legislature was to convene. He told Arnett he would be glad to do anything for Arnett he could. Arnett said he wanted the university in Boulder and had three hundred head of horses on his land, promising one to his old friend Topping. When Topping cast the deciding vote, Boulder had its university.

A. J. Macky, one of Boulder's early day citizens, helped lead the drive that raised money to establish the University of Colorado in Boulder. (From Bixby, *History of Clear Creek and Boulder Valleys*)

Topping laughed, stood up in the House, and said, "I've got a horse!"

The legislature appropriated $15,000 for a University of Colorado at Boulder "conditioned upon the subscription of a similar sum by Boulder citizens." Boulder had just raised matching funds for the railroad in 1872-73, but once again the old guard stepped forward. Andrew Macky, Marinus Smith, and David Nichols led a drive that raised $16,806.33 with donations ranging from $15 to $1000. Arnett donated five acres of land for the present campus and $500 and also gave the university another eighty acres north of Lover's Hill (Sunset Hill) which were subsequently purchased from the state by C. M. Tyler.

George Andrews contributed land, and Marinus Smith, who came to Boulder with $2 and a horse in 1859, gave twenty-five acres, five interests in the Anderson Ditch, and $1020 in cash. Years later Smith's daughter, Sarah Tourtellot, told her friend Louisa Montgomery of the Montgomery House on Pearl, "Everybody thought he was crazy, Lou. All that land at the foot of the mountains, barren, rocky, a hill sloping down to the creek bed. A university site! Whoever—well, it just wasn't to be thought of!"

Hale Scientific Building and Old Main on the University of Colorado campus. (*Boulder Historical Society*)

But it was to be, and it is no wonder that a bronze tablet was placed on the university campus, "In Memory of Marinus Gilbert Smith, George Asa Andrews and Anthony Arnett, Citizens of Boulder, who in 1872, when the University of Colorado was still a dream, donated the land upon which it was to begin its life."

The cornerstone of Old Main was laid in September 1875, and, although its roof and one tower were blown off by high winds in February 1876, the university opened its doors on September 5, 1877, to its first entering class.

It must have been a little less charming than the beautiful campus of today. Jane Sewall, daughter of the university's first president, Joseph A. Sewall, wrote of her first view of Old Main: "It loomed before us gaunt and alone in the pitiless clear light. No tree nor shrub nor any human habitation was in sight. Vast expanses of rock and sagebrush were its only surrounding."

Oscar E. Jackson, one of the students in the first entering class, recalled that "a naked, ill-constructed building situated in a barren waste and removed from any sidewalk by nearly a mile of mud, was all that marked the place for a future University. . . ." It was surrounded by "pasture, pig pens, chicken coops, a barn, a horse shed and a wire fence to keep out the black bull that ruled the 12th Street region as late as 1889."

As bleak and muddy as it may have been, the arrival of the university forever altered the course of Boulder. As the founders had hoped, a new kind of citizenry began to arrive. A long stream of visitors came to visit President Sewall and the university. Where once ox-teams hauled their way through the streets and miners had planned for a long cold winter, there were music recitals, debates, and poetry readings. Boulder stores, for so long oriented towards the needs of the miners, now began to have advertisements for suits, boots, and university noteheads for the students and faculty. No longer would Boulder have to aspire "to be a 'city' in virtue of being a 'distributing point' for the settlements up the Boulder Canyon," as found by Isabella Bird in 1873; Boulder was on its way to becoming one of the intellectual centers of the entire West.

First Class Funerals and Famous Guests

Spurred on by such developments, Boulder began to get a little cocky. Not only was "Boulder City" a thing of the past, "Beautiful Boulder" now came to the fore. In 1875 a letter to the *Denver Daily News* signed by O.C. Casional spoke proudly of Boulder as "our beautiful town" and the way "public spirit and enterprise has taken hold of the people." Writing in 1941, Timothy William Stanton recalled that Boulder "was called 'Beautiful Boulder' then as it is now."

Of course, the local paper could be counted on to be wildly adamant and duly prejudiced about its home town:

> Ever and anon is heard the cry in Boulder that it has too many old fogies, that its business men lack enterprise, that the town needs some first class funerals, and remarks similarly entertaining, instructive and respectful.
> When the town had but a handful of people its enterprise and

liberality secured the construction of the B.V. road and the C.C. spirit, to borrow the idea of Mr. Bixby, then crowded out the wheelbarrow spirit and the town took a step forward. Following on the heels of this a handful of men, scarce a hundred we believe, raised eighteen thousand dollars to secure the State University near the limits of this town. Was this not liberality? Was this not enterprise?

Instead of having old fogies here we have a more go ahead, energetic, enterprising and charitable disposed set of men than can be found in any town of its size, east or west.

But while Boulder's nature and image were changing, life on the outlying farms was not. Looking back from 1941, C.F. Bennett remembered his early days on a homestead south of the Little Thompson about five miles north of Longmont. He thought of the simple cabin where he and his brothers and sisters were born and reflected upon how his twin brother had died at birth. Those were the days when most kids went to school on a "Rocky Mountain canary," a burro, and there was the day the animal became belligerent, bucking him all the way home and breaking his arm.

Worst of all were the grasshoppers. They wiped out the Wellmans' turnips back in 1860, and school teacher Abner Brown remembered their arrival in September 1861: ". . . suddenly the sky was darkened to almost the gloom of a total eclipse of the sun, and great drops of hail seemed to be driven against the windows and roof of the house. On looking out, we saw, to our astonishment and terror, that a perfect living cloud of full-grown grasshoppers filled the air in every direction, as far as the eye could reach. This scourge continued, settling down upon our fields and gardens as the cool of evening came on, until, with all we could do, by whipping the ground with brush, we could not make them rise more than a few inches above the ground, and, as we drove them before us in little jumps, by dark they were gathered into windrows of fifty feet in length and three to four inches deep."

One way to fight them was to use the irrigation ditches on the sides of the field. Bottles of kerosene would be placed along the bank with lamp wicks to carry the oil to the water, covering it in a film. The grasshoppers would jump in and be killed by the kerosene.

"We gathered them in bushels that way," wrote Stanton. "Late in the summer [1875] a new crop of flying grasshoppers came in such quantities that they would darken the sun, and we fought them off the garden by whipping them off."

C.F. Bennett remembered times when his mother worked all day in the fields driving grasshoppers toward a ditch. Even without grasshoppers, the farmer's day lasted "from as quick as you could see in the morning until you couldn't see at night," according to O.C. Bolton, whose family arrived in 1879. Bolton did a lot of threshing and baling in his day, but, even if it was hard, he looked back fondly at the "thrill [of] seeing the big steam engine pulling the crossed belt, the separator shooting out the golden straw." He also remembered with warmth "the big meals of wholesome food put up by the farm wives, the camaraderie of neighbors getting together."

And even in Bolton's time there was a longing for the good old days when quality hadn't succumbed to mass production: "I used to raise barley and haul it into the Crystal Springs Brewery, over here at 10th and Arapahoe. Four tons at a time. They used to wouldn't buy any barley that wasn't a year old. Now they'll take it right direct from the combine. . . . Maybe that's what's the matter with the beer."

The Crystal Springs Brewery began as the Boulder City Brewing Company in 1876. It supplied the mining camps, coal towns, and Boulder's ten saloons. The beer garden on the grounds, shaded by grape arbors and cottonwoods, with a trout pond as well, was one of the local showplaces. Before falling to Prohibition in 1916, the brewery produced up to a million barrels of beer per year.

The brewery was but one of several new businesses that were opening in Boulder during this decade in which the population grew from 343 to over 3000. Another sign of the times was the arrival of Charles Boettcher, whose success would lead to the well-known Boettcher Foundation of to-

The Crystal Springs Brewery, originally the Boulder City Brewing Company, was one of Boulder's leading businesses before it fell to prohibition in 1916. (*Boulder Historical Society*)

day. Boettcher came to Boulder from Fort Collins in 1872 and opened a hardware store on the corner of Broadway and Pearl. Soon he left his brother in charge of the store and went to Leadville, where he opened another store that was grossing $40,000 a month by 1882. Once, however, looking back on the four and one-half years he spent in Boulder, Boettcher called them "the happiest years of my life."

The growth of the '70s did wonders for the development of Boulder's early hotels. Boulder's first hotel, the Boulder House, was located at Eleventh and Pearl, originating as a log cabin in 1859. When the Squires and Tourtellot families bought the property in 1860, the wives cut willows and made them into brooms to sweep the dirt floor of the cabin-hotel. They watched the antelope drink peacefully from the creek, and when it rained they covered everything with horse blankets because of the leaky splint roof. In 1874 Thomas C. Brainard raised local eyebrows when he spent $6000 to remodel the hotel, spending $2700 on furniture alone. As the *News* remarked, "the carpets costly, the beds

Lobby of the Boulder House, Boulder's first hotel.
(*Boulder Historical Society*)

The German House at Eighth and Pearl. (*Boulder Historical Society*)

furnished with springs, and mattresses with cotton tops. The appointments . . . are as complete as experience and expense can make them."

Boulder's next oldest hotel was the Colorado House at Thirteenth and Pearl. The site was purchased by Daniel Pound for $335.10 in 1863 and consisted of a two-story building with a one-story store attached. It too began to spruce up a bit, boasting "warm meals at all hours," with J. W. Brown, "the cook par excellence," in 1872.

The American House opened in the '70s, as did the Lund and German Houses. The German House, on the west end of Boulder at Eighth and Pearl, was popular with Germans, while the Lund catered mostly to Swedes. The hotel became known for its gooseberries, cold beer, and white picket fence.

Anthony Arnett opened the Arnett Hotel in 1867. It was located opposite the present offices of the *Boulder Daily Camera*, and when it was christened by a ball on Christmas Eve, it was described as being "one of the largest and most substantial buildings ever erected in this town." In 1875 it became the Sherman House and was designed to attract tourists. The rooms were heated by small stoves in each room and were lighted by lamps. Since there was no running water, the porter would bring a pitcher up in the morning. The rate was $3 a day for room and board. A fire in the room cost 25¢ extra.

There was no bathroom or toilet. All needs were tended to by a "Chick Sales Three Holer" on the alley, marked "Men" on one side and "Ladies" on the other. Arnett took over the hotel again in 1876, and one of his lessees boasted that there were sets of rooms they would not be ashamed to offer to President Grant and his wife. On August 21, 1880, President Grant arrived and registered at the hotel, then known as the Brainard. The Brainard also hosted P.T. Barnum and Tom Thumb and his wife, who rode around town in a tiny carriage drawn by Shetland ponies.

One other interesting visitor to Boulder around this time was Ward Lamon, who had once been Abraham Lincoln's law partner. Lamon stood well over six feet and weighed over 300 pounds, mined at Gold Hill and Magnolia, and actually resided in Boulder for awhile. Lincoln appointed him U.S. Marshal for the District of Columbia, and he was urged by the editors of the *Boulder News and Courier* to run for U.S. Senator from Colorado.

Lamon used to tell stories about his days with Lincoln, and one of these found its way into an article written by Carl Sandburg for *Redbook* in 1936. Much to Lincoln's disbelief, Lamon had often feared for the president's life. On one occasion Lincoln told Lamon how he had been riding home the preceding evening when a rifle shot went off not fifty yards away. Lincoln heard the bullet whistle by "at an uncomfortably short distance" but still couldn't believe anyone had shot or would deliberately shoot to kill him. Lincoln discussed the matter lightly, making more fuss over the panic of his horse and his wild ride rather than make something out of what may have been nothing.

"I do not want it understood that I share your apprehensions," he told Lamon. "I never have."

". . . I believe it is the inalienable right of man . . . to be happy or miserable at his own election," Lincoln added, to which Lamon replied: "Unless you are more careful and discreet, in less than a week you'll have neither inalienable nor any other rights. The time may not be distant when this republic will be minus a pretty respectable President."

The time came of course, and sixteen years later President Garfield was assassinated as well, shot by Charles Guitteau in Washington. By chance, Boulder had a remote association with this event also; Guitteau's former wife, who had remarried prior to the assassination, had lived here briefly before moving on to Leadville.

Boulder's old hotels, like so much else from the frontier days, have long since gone. Remodeled, moved, eventually razed, they marked an era and then made way for something else to come along. One of the last to go was the Arlington at 2121 Broadway. Originally the Sale, the hotel dated back to the '70s when the Sales claimed to have the first bath tub in Boulder and offered a free bus to and from all the trains. The

Sale promised free hot and cold baths to guests at rates of $1.40 per day.

When the hotel was razed in 1965, Forest Crossen wrote a story for the *Camera*, which he heard from George P. Sale, son of the founder of the old hotel. It was late in the 1870s. George Sale, then a young boy, was in the lobby of the hotel when four strangers walked in and asked for a room. Sale's mother had spent some time in Kentucky and knew that the strangers were the James gang: Jesse, Frank, and Bob Ford and his brother. The men were roughly dressed and looked like they had just finished a long ride. Sale's father led them upstairs to a back room.

After a little nap they called downstairs for the young boy, and George Sale went up to their room. "I was kinda timid when I knocked on the door of No. 13," Sale said. "The

The Sale Hotel claimed to have Boulder's first bath tub. Late in the 1870s it hosted Frank and Jesse James. (*Boulder Historical Society*)

leader invited me inside. I glanced around the room, my eyes wide. They had more rifles and six-shooters and ammunition lying around than I had ever seen. They were handsome, friendly men, and their smiles took away my fear.

" 'What do you think of our outfit for a hunting trip across the Range?' asked Jesse James, smiling.

" 'All right,' I answered him. Like all boys I admired guns. 'You've got some good guns there.'

" 'You're right,' said Jesse," and then he asked the young Sale to run an errand for him. When Sale returned with a small package, Jesse gave him a dollar tip, which was more money than I had ever made in my life."

Sale took a quick liking to the generous men, who always tipped him a dollar for running an errand. The Jameses and Fords stayed several days at the hotel, visiting with the family, talking about the old days in Kentucky and remembering when Mrs. Sale's father had given them shelter. Sometimes a family from Missouri would stop in to visit and tell whether any local police officers were around. One of the four would always stay in the room when the others went out for a walk around town. One day George's father and Jesse James were walking west on Pearl from Twelfth Street when he stopped, stared at a stranger, and let his right hand streak to his hip.

" 'You looking for me?' he asked coldly. 'If you are, here I am.'

"Father said for a long moment the men stared at each other. Then the stranger dropped his eyes and moved on.

" 'That man's a detective who's been trailing me,' Jesse explained.

"That night the James boys and the Fords rode out of Boulder, telling us a last goodbye. We never saw them again. I don't think they were ever in Boulder again."

A few years later, in 1882, Bob Ford shot and killed Jesse James to claim the reward offered by the governor of Missouri. Ten years later he fell to a shotgun blast fired by Ed Kelly in the mining camp of Creede.

PART III
End of the Frontier

The departure of Jesse James marked the end of an era in Boulder. He may have been on the wrong side of the law, but Jesse James was synonymous with the wild days of the west. A notorious outlaw who lived and died by the gun, he was of an era when a man made his own way or didn't make it at all. Municipal water supplies, sewage problems, ordinances—these were not part of Jesse James' life, nor were they of great concern to Boulder's first pioneers. Their reasons may have differed, but neither the pioneers nor Jesse James had time for such civilized matters.

By 1883 "Boulder was still a small town with much of the rawness of the frontier about it," according to one observer, but Boulder's future was no longer in doubt. Boulder was a legally organized city in a recently created state. It had banks, hotels, railroads, more churches than some believed it could support, a county courthouse, university, businesses, doctors, lawyers, and newspapers.

An additional sign of Boulder's sense of certainty was the formation of the Society of Boulder Pioneers in 1883 "to collect and preserve information connected with the early settlement and subsequent history of the county, and to perpetuate the memory of those whose sagacity, energy and enterprise induced them to settle in the wilderness and helped to become the founders of a new state and county." We can say with some certainty that cities and towns don't bother preserving their past when no future seems to lie ahead.

Boulder of the 1880s was settled and sitting back to refine itself. It was a decade in which the population inched slowly from 3,069 to 3,330. Its institutions in place and the Indians gone, Boulder spent ten years establishing water extensions and arguing over temperance and prohibition. Boulder built a city hall, acquired a jail, and established grades for streets. A board of trade was organized. Whittier School was built in 1882. Mapleton School opened in 1889. Street lights came along, and so did an outbreak of smallpox and the opening of the Silver Lake Ditch. The year 1885 was highlighted by the state firemen's tournament; 1886 saw the formation of the Boulder Library Association and more water extensions.

In lighter moments Boulder would enjoy watching its world championship fire hose team or reading about the latest problems with prostitution at the end of Water Street (Canyon Boulevard), where the Public Library and Municipal Building now stand.

Prostitution was hardly a laughing matter, as far as most of the town was concerned. Boulder's Board of Trustees passed an ordinance prohibiting prostitution in 1873, but by the 1880s there were at least five houses operating in the red light district. Even the old schoolhouse, which gave way to Central School in 1873, was being used as a bordello. In 1886 the editor of the *Boulder County Herald* reflected the popular disgust with prostitution and the image it was creating: "The first thing a person sees on lighting from the cars in Boulder and the last seen on getting on the train are these institutions of infamy."

From the 1880s until the early 1900s, the newspapers were dotted with stories of Madam Kingsley, Trixie Lee, Sue Brown, Molly Gordon, and Mountain Pink. There were periodic raids and fines, hiding of "the boys" names because they came from "good and respected families," and continued public concern. Finally, in 1897, the Citizen's Reform League met and passed a resolution to make Boulder "the cleanest and purest city within the state." A dispute developed over whether prostitution could ever be eradicated or simply localized and controlled, but the culminating blow came with prohibition, reform, and the arrival of Billy Sunday. The days were gone when Boulder would wake up to find that a fight had broken out at Madam Kingsley's and she was found defending herself with a ten-

Boulder in 1889. With churches and schools, a courthouse, and a university, it was no longer a frontier town. (*Boulder Historical Society*)

inch carving knife, or that one of her girls had been shot and killed by an angry wife. No longer would there be stories about some poor "soiled dove" who had tried to commit suicide or died from an overdose of cocaine. While such things are hardly necessary to the existence of a successful community, their presence was part of a colorful era that was slipping away. Martin Parsons probably wasn't the only pioneer who looked back on the success of the reform movement and lamented, "The town's never been any good since."

While such women provided gaudy counterpoint to the restrained tones of the times, there were other women who played significant roles in leading Boulder out of the frontier period and into the modern era.

When Mary Rippon came to teach at the university, she became the first woman in the United States to teach at a state university. She spent fifty-seven years as professor of French and German and was instrumental in the establishment of a public library in Boulder. The university's Mary Rippon Theater is named in her honor. Hannah Connell Barker, another woman of keen intellect, was one of Boulder's first teachers and spent an active life in various civic and philanthropic activities ranging from the women's literary Fortnightly group to beautifying Columbia Cemetery. She gave park land, served as director of the Boulder National Bank, and joined other women in starting the Boulder Creamery Company in 1887. An active Congregationalist, she helped write the church's history and donated half of the money needed for the church to buy an organ.

Several women practiced medicine during these times, one of whom, Dr. Mary Solander, became the first woman inmate in the prison at Canon City. Although there was much dispute over whether Dr. Solander was guilty, she was convicted of manslaughter after allegedly performing an abortion on a woman in Left Hand and spent a few months of her five-year sentence before being released.

One of the most interesting early Boulder women was diminutive Martha Dartt Maxwell, who earned a national reputation as a skilled taxidermist. Her grandfather taught her how to shoot, and she learned the rudiments of taxidermy from a German squatter on the Maxwell property near Boulder. Family finances caused her to sell her first collection of 1200 animals to Shaw's Botanical Gardens in St. Louis, but she began a new collection that was exhibited with much success at the Philadelphia Exposition of 1876.

A photograph of Martha Maxwell against a painted backdrop, dressed in a buckskin and carrying a rifle, calls to mind the one person who most represents Boulder's final transition from frontier to modern times: Joseph Bevier Sturtevant, popularly known as "Rocky Mountain Joe."

By the time he arrived in Boulder in 1876, Rocky Mountain Joe had been raised by Indians in Wisconsin, joined the circus in Cairo, Illinois, and fought with the 4th Wisconsin Cavalry. He had survived capture by a band of Sitting Bull's warriors and had made a walking tour of Florida. He had fought with Custer in 1873 and gone with Colonel Cook later in the year, where he acquired the nickname of Rocky Mountain Joe. Had he not been sent on a different mission at the time, he would have died with Custer at the Little Big Horn.

All this made quite a colorful background for a man who arrived in Boulder as a paper hanger and painter of homes and signs. On December 19, 1876, Sturtevant married Anna Lyckman and built a small house on the present site of 744 Marine Street for $100. In 1880 he published a book of engravings entitled "Scenes of Boulder and Vicinity," and in 1884 he went back east, returning with some photographic equipment. On March 20, 1889 the *Boulder County Herald* reported that Sturtevant had found what is still one of the earliest known photographs of Boulder, a picture of Pearl Street taken in 1866:

"In the rubbish at a second-hand store Jos. Sturtevant found an old photograph, which he would not sell for $20. It was taken in Boulder in 1866. The first house in the foreground is the old Colorado House. In the enclosure to the west is a pig stye. Then comes a frame shanty now occupied

"Boulder, 1866," found in rubbish at a secondhand store by J. B. Sturtevant, is the oldest known picture of Boulder. (*Boulder Historical Society*)

by the Chinese laundry. The next building is the Macky-Dabney block. Beyond this are two small frame shanties, and then the western portion of the Boulder House. The eastern portion had not then been built on. Beyond this are the mountains. No other business houses or dwelling houses appear.

"In front of the Colorado House stand a low wagon and some women and men. The women wore balloon hoopskirts then, and the men had on long baggy coats. It is not known to whom the picture belongs, but Jos. claims it now. Chas. Dabney says he remembers when the picture was taken, that it was in '66 and it is now over 22 years old."

Sturtevant went on to take thousands of pictures in and around Boulder over the years. With his Buffalo Bill hair style and fringed buckskin clothes, the dashing Rocky Mountain Joe was a well-known Boulder personality and became the photographer in residence when the Texas-Colorado Chautauqua opened in 1899.

Boulder's Chautauqua was the logical culmination of the realization that Boulder's climate and setting offered great possibilities for a resort. As early as 1874 we have a record of a visitor to Boulder Canyon gasping in wonder: "It would

Indian fighter, paperhanger, painter, and photographer, J. B. Sturtevant,
"Rocky Mountain Joe," was one of Boulder's most colorful figures.
(Boulder Historical Society)

The Sanitarium, now Boulder Memorial Hospital, once stood alone at the mouth of Sunshine Canyon. (*Boulder Historical Society*)

seem that here is the studio of nature where scenes that far excel all works of man's pencil are hung with lavish profusion upon the granite walls."

Many more comments extolling Boulder's natural advantages followed, and in 1893 Elder John Fulton of the Seventh Day Adventists, in Colorado for his health, wrote to Dr. J.H. Kellogg urging that a sanitarium be established in Boulder. Dr. Kellogg was then superintendant of the Battle Creek Sanitarium, begun by the church in Battle Creek, Michigan in 1866. A facility was opened in Boulder in a boarding house in December "to offer invalids and those needing rest and recuperation under favorable circumstances the superior advantages of the Sanitarium board and treatment in connection with homelike surroundings." Early in 1895 the Sanitarium acquired about ninety acres for an expanded facility, which became the forerunner of today's Boulder Memorial Hospital.

It was during these years that a group of Texas school teachers became interested in building "a summer school in a climate where health and comfort predominate, and amidst surroundings which tend to the highest development of the mind."

Boulder welcomed the interest of the Texans as warmly as

it had received the Congregationalists thirty years before, purchasing a park a mile and a half from town and erecting a 5000 seat auditorium at a cost of $10,000. Private cottages were built and soon patrons were coming from a dozen states to spend their summers in Boulder, hear lectures, take excursions in the mountains, and be photographed by Rocky Mountain Joe. The management was quick to point out that it would "make every effort to provide cottages, tents or rooms to all who apply," and that, because of its fencing and police force, "This spot is one of the safest in America for a man to send his family."

The Texas-Colorado Chautauqua opened in the summer of 1898, and by 1899 an electric railway connected the grounds with Boulder. The fare was 5¢, and the route proceeded "along the base of the mountains to one of the grandest landscape scenes on the continent." A 12x14 tent, with floor, cost $11 for the season; tent flies $2.50. Cottages were $15 and up. Board was $5 a week, and daily calls by a

The streetcar to Chautauqua, by "Rocky Mountain" Joe Sturtevant. (*Boulder Historical Society*)

grocer, baker, butcher, milkman, and other purveyors promised a meeting of all family needs.

The arrival of Chautauqua brought some of the first references to the "Flatirons" as the name for Boulder's striking faces of rock. Although Captain Aikens' party had referred to Sunset Rock, because of the way the most northern Flatiron caught the last of the autumn sun, the name didn't catch on. Sturtevant, who photographed the Flatirons many times, called them the "Chautauqua Slabs" and Junius Henderson, a Boulder attorney, called them the "Towering Pinnacles" in 1903. By then Chautauqua bulletins were using the name "Flatirons," but we still don't know the origin for sure. One guess is that the word originated because of the similarity to pressing devices called "sadirons" which were used at the time. Another suggestion is that they were named because of the Flatirons Building in New York City, a skyscraper built in the 1890s. Since the building increased wind turbulence at its corner of Fifth Avenue and Broadway, one student of the problem feels there may be a real possibility to this explanation.

One of the great attractions in Boulder at the turn of the century was to ride the train to Ward along the Switzerland Trail, which seemed to rise briefly as one magnificent, final reminder of Boulder's vanished frontier.

For the most part, the story of the railroad in and around Boulder lacks the drama and excitement of railroading in the Rockies with its unending tales of blasting through rock, building trestles over great gorges, and passengers holding their breath as the train hugged a cliff on its way to an isolated town. In Boulder the only perseverance required lay in getting the railroad to extend its tracks from Erie into town. With the Switzerland Trail, however, we find much of the color and excitement that is associated with railroading in Colorado.

In 1883 the Union Pacific began an ambitious project west out of Boulder called the Greeley, Salt Lake & Pacific. Falling somewhat short of expectations, the railroad made it only as far as Sunset, twelve miles out of Boulder, and then

The Switzerland Trail wound its way up past the old mines into the high country, offering a fine day's outing and splendid views, most of the time. (*Boulder Historical Society*)

was washed away by the flood of 1894. In 1898 the Colorado and Northern followed the old route up Boulder and Four Mile canyons, climbed beyond Sunset to Gold Hill and Brainard, and stopped at Ward. A branch built in 1905 ran south from Sunset to Sugarloaf, Glacier Lake, and Eldora.

Originally contemplated as a freight line, the railroad showed great attraction to the public as a tourist trip, and management was quick to capitalize, coining the name, "The Switzerland Trail of America." *The Switzerland Trail Guide Book* of 1904 described how the railroad wound like a great snake, crossing Boulder Creek under Profile Rock, up toward Arapaho Peak, Long's Peak, the Divide, and round the Ox-Bow, climbing 3500' in sixteen miles. At Mont Alto Park you reached another ascent, shorter curves, and higher mountains. "(I)n the valley the stream and wagon road have become mere threads, the cabins only children's toys. Groups of mines appear, taking the traveler's attention." Bald Mountain came into view. California Gulch lay below. Finally the train reached Ward, which promised to be "one of the best mining camps in the state. A very sociable and intelligent class of people reside there. Every branch of mercantile business is represented. Ward is a paradise for tourists and campers in the summer."

Proud, exaggerated, inflated, the tone of the guide book was fully justified; only forty years before, most had agreed Boulder Canyon alone was totally impassable.

Spurred on by the railroad, Chautauqua, the development of Boulder as a resort center, and even a brief oil boom in 1891, Boulder's population nearly doubled to 6,150 in the '90s, and the county population reached 20,000.

Boulder in the '80s and '90s had become "no more or less than a typical frontier town," according to Prof. W.H. Burger, who had been a native resident. Most of the houses were of wood; few of the old log buildings remained. There were a few rough stone buildings and uneven wooden sidewalks. Kids and adults would fish for coins dropped through the wooden cracks, and when the cracks were filled with tar the kids would work it out on hot days and make tar

balls. In winter kids would skate and sled, flying down
Mapleton Hill all the way to Fifteenth Street on "jumpers,"
a broad curved stave from a whiskey barrel with a short post
nailed to the stave and a cross piece for the rider to sit on.
These were the days of kerosene street lights and night
baseball, stage lines and saloons, the circus, fairs, and a
Boulder band.

Presaging a later day with its Pearl Street Mall, the town
also sported street fakirs and ventriloquists who performed
for the public, trying to sell cure-alls, hair restoratives,
various medicines, and belts that could cure rheumatism.

There were other issues that sound strikingly familiar to
our own time. In the 1890s a conflict broke out between
preservationists and developers, or between those who
wanted to keep Boulder quiet and beautiful and those who
wished to see the development of industries with attractive
payrolls. When a prospective industrialist met a lukewarm
welcome in 1891, the *Camera* remonstrated, "Boulder must
have factories and the only way to get them is to seize them
when in sight. Sugar catches more flies than vinegar, and
billious traitors to their own city and to their own families
should be weeded out." A few years later the *Camera*
became a little more succinct: "A regular payroll is what
Boulder wants. For it is written that man cannot live upon
climate alone."

Yet another issue which rings familiarly in the contemporary ear is the financial crisis of 1899 that almost brought
an end to the university. After the Panic of '93 money was
scarce in Colorado, and special appropriations by the legislature were rare. The university was supported by a mill levy
of 1/5 mill, a land fund, and special appropriations. In 1898-
1900 the legislature voted $220,000 worth of special approp-
riations for the university, but because of financial conditions not a dollar arrived. A citizens' committee formed, and
the *Camera*, citing the importance of the university to the
city, urged community support. Warrants were issued, pro-
fessors contributed from their salaries, and banks gave
loans. At Christmas 1899 people in Boulder and Denver

raised $60,000 to buy coal and make token salaries to professors. Finally, reacting to aroused citizens, the legislature voted a special appropriation of $80,000, which the university received. It would not be the last time the university would find itself mired in battle with the legislature over some aspect of its existence.

The times sound familiar to our own, although in numbers of years they were far closer to the days of the frontier. Yet, while there is a similarity to the flavor of life in the 1860s and 1870s compared with that of the 1880s and 1890s, the recollections of Prof. Burger seem quite removed from the years of Indian scares and the days when a boy spent his afternoon chasing antelope on a horse, relishing the "rare delicious taste" of an apple that was divided among his family, caulking a floor with thin strips of wool, or banking up the outside of the house with manure that would be removed in the spring.

Reflecting upon the early years from his vantage point of 1879, Rev. Nathan Thompson wrote to the *Boulder County News*, "It used to be in my mind when with you to talk up and form a Boulder County Historical Society. Has it been done yet? It ought to be. Lead off, some of you, and gather in the history of the pens of pioneers before it is too late.

"The unbridged creek, the old school house and its lyceums, the first printing press, even the street corners have volumes to tell us. Yes, lead off. A hundred years hence, thousands will have heart-felt thanks for it."

Thirty years later, in 1909, the Pioneer Society held its annual meeting, and Aunty Brookfield reigned as queen over the semi-centennial celebration of the days of '59. Although many of the pioneers had moved away or died, many were still present to reminisce, visit old friends, and recall the days of the past. It is through their letters, diaries, and journals that much of what we know of frontier Boulder has come down to us.

But ultimately history is not a matter of names and dates, or a collection of artifacts and journals. It is a sense of time and place, a feeling for what has been combined with an awareness of how it affects what is and may be.

Today Boulder is a far cry from what it once was; it is now a bustling city that draws national attention for reasons far removed from silver or gold. The pioneers would hardly recognize their old Red Rocks, but they would probably be amused to see how we struggle, through blue lines and green belts, growth plans and historic preservation laws, to preserve the very qualities they once knew.

Predictions are that Boulder is destined to become a home for "high tech" industries and an intellectual center of the West. "Of course," the oldtimers would reply, "we called Boulder 'the Athens of the West' a long time ago."

We change but don't change, dream on but look back. In Boulder we find certainty only in our great rock slabs, awful winds, and deep blue skies. We know only that thousands more will come, look down into the valley and decide to stay because "the mountains looked right." And we can feel that in some way, not obvious or pervasive, all that we ever do here will somehow be affected by the dreams and events of those who arrived first.

PART IV
The Sites Today

The amazing thing about the upper picture on the opposite page is not that the house still stands but that its address is 2940 20th Street. Built in 1875 by Judge J.H. Decker and bought that year by Captain Clinton M. Tyler, this farmhouse once stood several miles outside of Boulder. Now it stands in the middle of a subdivision in the heart of the city. Where once were groves of trees and open farm land, now there are rows of houses, paved streets, and cars. Perhaps no single picture more graphically shows the change in Boulder over the past 100 years than this old photo.

There are other places in Boulder where the changes have been dramatic. At the corner of 35th and Moorhead, at 15 South 35th Street, you will find the *Martin Farmhouse*, built around 1875 by William "Billy" Martin, one of the discoverers of the great Caribou mine. In the 1860s the property was a campsite for prospectors on their way to the mines. Later, stagecoaches and wagons stopped by to enjoy the spring that once supplied all the home's domestic water. Originally surrounded by 400 acres of land, the property, except for the lots of the original home, was sold in the 1950s and developed into what we now know as Martin Acres.

Although many of Boulder's early homes and buildings have been lost over the years, Boulder is fortunate in that a great number still stand. These have been described in various recent works, but we might note quickly a few of the sites today that are pertinent to frontier Boulder.

At 646 Pearl Street, for example, is the quaint little *Arnett-Fullen House*, a Victorian gingerbread structure with a two-story French Mansard tower. The house was built in 1876-1877 by Anthony Arnett, who wanted it to excel "any residence ever before erected in Boulder." The iron cresting and elaborate wrought iron were supposedly brought from Omaha by ox-cart.

The Tyler House, once the heart of a farm surrounded by trees and land, now stands, well-preserved, in the middle of a thriving subdivision. (*Boulder Public Library*)

The Arnett-Fullen house, 646 Pearl, was built in 1876-1877. (*Richard L. Fetter*)

The *Brookfield House* is also still here. Alfred A. Brookfield, one of Boulder's founders, and "Aunty" Brookfield, queen of the bicentennial celebration of 1909, lived at 1840 Walnut in a home built by pioneer Amos Widner in 1874 when he subdivided his farm. The Brookfields bought the home in 1889. It is located just across Nineteenth Street to the west of the September School.

The little gray *Culver-Bixby House* at 1733 Canyon Boulevard was built in 1871. Culver brought out the first steam quartz mill to Boulder. Bixby, who bought the house in 1871, owned the *Boulder County News* and wrote *History of Clear Creek and Boulder Valleys*, one of Boulder's first histories. Appropriately enough, this old structure now serves as the home of Historic Boulder.

The *Squires-Tourtellot House*, built in 1865 by Boulder pioneers Frederick A. Squires and Jonathan Tourtellot, is believed to be Boulder's oldest house. Maria Tourtellot and Miranda Squires, twin sisters, worked with their merchant husbands and lived in the front half of a double cabin at

The Squires-Tourtellot House, now Boulder's oldest house, is the home of the Boulder Historical Society. (*Boulder Historical Society*)

The Affolter-Dodd cabin, built in 1860, is the oldest cabin in Boulder County. (*Richard L. Fetter*)

Eleventh and Pearl when they first arrived. The fine house at 1019 Spruce, built solidly of stone, must have been a change from the leaky roofs and dirt floors that typified the times. Today the house serves as the home of the Boulder Historical Society, with its excellent collection of photographs, clothing, and other artifacts from Boulder's past.

To find the oldest cabin in Boulder County, you will have to go to Longmont and visit the *Affolter-Dodd Cabin*, now located in Old Mill Park at 237 Pratt Street, a few blocks west of Main. The young Affolter brothers, Jacob and Frederick, left Switzerland in 1852 and built their cabin on Left Hand Creek, just south of Haystack Mountain, in 1860. In 1970 the Dodd brothers, descendants of a local pioneer family, donated the cabin to the St. Vrain Historical Society, which restored the structure in Old Mill Park. Dedication ceremonies were held on August 1, 1976. The old cabin was allegedly used by the Hayden Survey on July 4, 1869.

Old Mill Park is a tiny gem of a site, well worth a visit by the traveler fond of local history. In addition to the Affolter-Dodd Cabin, the park is the home of an old mill, another old cabin, and the *Hauck Milk House*, which was built around 1860 by Robert A. Hauck on land given to him by Chief Niwot. Hauck established one of the first farms in the St. Vrain Valley and helped build the first cabin in Boulder City and the first rural school in Colorado Territory. His stone milk house was dismantled, moved, and restored in Old Mill Park by the Territorial Daughters of Colorado and the Colorado State Society of the Daughters of the American Revolution. It was dedicated on Colorado's Centennial Day, August 1, 1976.

While you are in Longmont, return to Main Street, turn left, and go to the corner of Fourth and Kimbark, where you will find a quartz stone that was part of the *first ore mill* in Boulder County. Once used at the Horsfal mine near Gold Hill, the stone now rests permanently on the west side of City Hall Annex on the southeast corner of the intersection, across from Longmont's Pioneer Museum.

If you are wondering why it is that these old buildings and the county's first quartz mill have wound up in Longmont even though they were once closer to Boulder, just recall that Boulder once stole Valmont's newspaper. History has its way of taking care of inequities.

As you leave Longmont, you might want to visit the old stone *Ryssby Church*, built in 1881-1882 as the First Lutheran Church in Colorado. It is on County Road 63, about six and a half miles southwest of Longmont.

Come back to Valmont and pick up 63rd Street, and you can find the marker for old *Fort Chambers*, 0.2 miles northeast of the town. This is where the 100′x150′ sod structure was built in 1864 during the height of the Indian scares. The *Chambers House* was another one-tenth of a mile away.

You must return to Boulder to find the oldest sites of historic interest in the area. The *First White Camp* is in Settler's Park on a hill above the junction of Canyon Boulevard and Pearl. Follow Pearl almost to where the two roads join and you will find the sign for the park. Walk up the short dirt path into the park and keep walking straight up the hill until you come to the plaque which commemorates the arrival of the Aikens-Brookfield party on October 17, 1858. Follow the path up the hill a little further and you will see *Red Rocks*, still as eye-catching and inspiring today as it must have been to the first pioneers. If much of Boulder has changed dramatically since their day, here is one place which has not. As you emerge from the trees onto the base of the small hill, only the path before you intrudes on the very scene they would have found.

Drive up Mapleton Hill toward the mouth of Sunshine Canyon, turn left into the Knollwood subdivision, and you can find *Gyp Rock*. Once you take the left off Mapleton, the road bends left again, bringing you toward a lovely home built against a large rock. This is Gyp Rock, and you can find a path that skirts the house to the south and leads around to the rock. Follow it right to the natural cleft that gives a view across to the greenbelt area on the north of Mapleton, and you will find the word GYP carved into the rock. Gyp Rock is on land that is privately owned, so take care that you confine your wanderings to the path and the rock itself. Wedge yourself in between the rocks, look south to the valley, the Flatirons and Red Rocks. Imagine an Indian with bow drawn, arrow pointing toward you, and you have what poor Gyp's last view would have been.

Another spot full of history is *Columbia Cemetery*, or Pioneer Cemetery, at Ninth and Pleasant. There have been no burials here since 1964, and the place has become somewhat of a park. The cemetery was begun around 1870. Its earliest readable headstone is dated 1871.

We would expect to find a number of sites along Pearl Street, this being one of Boulder's original streets, and there are. The log cabins disappeared a long time ago, as did the *Arnett Hotel*, which was opposite the Daily Camera offices at 1025 Pearl. But as you proceed onto the mall you come to the *Boulder City Building* at 1136 Pearl, which was built in 1882 and has seen a variety of uses in its century of existence.

In the same block, standing prominently at the corner of Pearl and Broadway, the *Boettcher Building* at 1144 Pearl clearly shows its date as 1878. Built by Charles Boettcher, the building lasted as a hardware store until 1973. Boettcher left Boulder in 1879 to become one of the wealthiest men in Colorado, founding such businesses as Great Western Sugar, Ideal Cement, and the first electric light and power plants in Leadville, Salt Lake City, and St. Louis.

Crossing Broadway, still on the mall, you come to the old *Fonda Drugstore*, now China Jones, at 1218 Pearl, built in 1889 by George P. Fonda, a Boulder druggist, alderman, and avid fire chief. The *Buckingham Building* (1899) at 1242 Pearl was Boulder's first permanent bank building and is Boulder's oldest business firm still in operation today. Started in 1874 by Charles G. and Walter A. Buckingham, the Buckingham Brothers Bank became the National State Bank of Boulder, and, more recently, the IntraWest Bank of Boulder. Finally, at 1408 Pearl, there is the *Boulder Hardware Building*, certainly an old timer (1895) although well past the time of the frontier.

Away from the mall, there is the *Congregational Church Bell* on the north side of the church at Fourteenth and Pine. It was brought out by ox team in 1869.

Other prominent sites include *Old Main* (1876) on the university campus and the *Boulder Depot* on Thirtieth Street. Built by the Union Pacific Railroad of locally quarried sandstone in 1890, the old depot was saved and restored by the Jaycees, who moved it to its present site in 1973.

Chautauqua is listed in the National Register of Historic Places. Located just off Baseline near the foot of the Flatirons, Boulder's Chautauqua is one of two remaining from the nineteenth century movement that began as a religious summer resort combining education and entertainment.

Boulder also has a wealth of early-day schools still in existence and use. *Central School* (1872), which replaced the original first school house in Colorado, was torn down in 1972, but *Whittier* (1883—formerly the *Pine Street School*) and *Mapleton* (1899) are still in use as schools. The *High-*

Fort St. Vrain Monument. Deer scurry past the site much as they might have in 1858 when the Aikens-Brookfield party arrived, climbed the fort's crumbling walls, and followed the streams to Boulder where "the mountains looked right." (*Richard L. Fetter*)

land School (1892) has been converted to offices, and *Mt. St. Gertrude Academy* (1892) at 970 Aurora was a boarding school for seventy-seven years. Now it is used for university offices.

Finally, however, you should drive out to the place from which the site of Boulder was first spotted so long ago, *Fort St. Vrain*. Take U.S. 285 north, past the restoration of Fort Vasquez, past the town of Platteville, to the little left-hand turn onto Highway 60. The road is paved, but you must take a left onto the well-maintained but dirt RD 40. Follow it 2.4 miles west and you will come to a little knoll and a stone monument that marks the site of old Fort St. Vrain. Francis Parkman once passed here, noting the crumbling old walls some twenty years before Aikens and Brookfield arrived. Since the walls are gone, you must content yourself with climbing up onto the new stone base of the marker. Look off to the southwest and you will find the shapes of Green Mountain and Bear Mountain rising in the distance above Boulder. In the early morning, if the angle of the sun is right, perhaps you can even pick out the rigid forms of the Flatirons. Here, so long ago, the first party paused, looked off as you are, and decided the mountains looked right. Surprisingly, today, from here little has changed. The valley still rolls toward the South Platte on its way to the Missouri. Here, where our story began, is a place to pause, to end, and to contemplate the time that was Frontier Boulder.

Sources

Newspapers

"Aunty Brookfield is Ninety-One Hale, Hearty and Jovial as Ever." *Boulder Daily Camera*, clipping, n.d.

Barker, Jane. "Boulder Society in 1869." *Focus. Boulder Daily Camera*, December 8, 1974.

_____. "A Ladies Literary Society is Formed." *Boulder Daily Camera*, clipping, n.d.

_____. "Boulder's First High School." *Focus. Boulder Daily Camera*, December 1, 1974.

_____. "Harold Stevens Remembers." *Focus. Boulder Daily Camera*, May 5, 1974.

_____. "A Martin Park Landmark." *Focus. Boulder Daily Camera*, March 20, 1977.

_____. "There Once Was A Brewery In Boulder." *Boulder Daily Camera*, March, 1978.

Bixby, Amos. "Red Rock Was The First Name Settlers Gave to What is Boulder." *Boulder Daily Camera*, clipping, n.d.

"Boulder, Colo. Historical Incidents." *Boulder Daily Camera*, August 22 and 31, 1931.

"Boulder, Colorado, Post Office History." *Boulder Daily Camera*, April 23 and 28, 1960.

"Boulder County and Its Resources." *Denver Tribune*, March 31, 1871.

"Boulder Salutes National State Bank on its 65th Anniversary." *Boulder Daily Camera*, April 21, 1939.

"Boulder's Congregational Church Organized in Cottonwood Grove in 1864." *Boulder Daily Camera*, July 16, 1954.

"Boulder's Old-Timer, Sam White, Celebrates his 104th Birthday." *Boulder Daily Camera*, May 19, 1965.

"Boulder's Only Hanging." *Boulder Daily Camera*, March 26, 1908.

Burger, W. H. "Boulder in '80s and '90s as Recalled by Prof. W. H. Burger, Native Resident." *Boulder Daily Camera*, July 31, 1945.

Butman, Beverly. "76 Year-Old Remembers Boulder Way Back When." *Boulder Daily Camera*, July 4, 1976.

"Charter Members Had Exciting Time Reaching Boulder." *Boulder Daily Camera*, April 26, 1935.

"Colorado's First Public School." *Boulder Daily Camera*, October 11, 1936.

Cornett, Linda. "Boulder's Ghosts." *Focus. Boulder Daily Camera*, October 23, 1977.

"Courthouse Cornerstone Laid July 4, 1882." *Boulder Daily Camera*, July 4, 1976.

Crossen, Forest. "Jesse James' Visit in Boulder Was Recalled by Son of Hosts." *Boulder Daily Camera*, August 14, 1965.

_____. "O.C. Bolton Recalls Earlier Days of Farm Life in Boulder, Colorado." *Boulder Daily Camera*, clipping, n.d.

_____. "Origin of Gunbarrel Hill Told by Albert Viele." *Boulder Daily Camera*, clipping, n.d.

_____. "Oldtimers Recall 'Indian Jack,' a Character of Earlier Boulder." *Boulder Daily Camera*, June 24, 1963.

Fritz, Percy S. "Mining History of Boulder County." *Boulder Daily Camera*, July 31, 1945.

"Ghost of Boulder's Hanging Tree." *Boulder County News*, May 15, 1874. *Boulder Daily Camera*, March 28, 1908.

Gladden, Sanford C. "Boulder's Early Churches." *Focus. Boulder Daily Camera*, September 29, 1979.

—————. "Boulder's First Hotel." *Focus. Boulder Daily Camera*, August 2, 1970.

—————. "Early Boulder Women Did More Than Feed Their Families." *Focus. Boulder Daily Camera*, January 7, 1979.

—————. "Early-day Mills Ground The Flour For Boulder's Bread." *Focus. Boulder Daily Camera*, February 10, 1980.

—————. "Memorial Hospital's Ancestry has Roots in Boarding House." *Focus. Boulder Daily Camera*, December 3, 1978.

"History of Boulder Library Grows With City." *Boulder Daily Camera*, November 11, 1961.

"Historic Ryssby Church Scene of Annual Festival Sunday." *Boulder Daily Camera*, June 19, 1954.

Knudsen, Larry. "When Prostitution Was An Issue." *Focus. Boulder Daily Camera*, March 11, 1973.

Lansford, Henry. "America's Switzerland Trail." *Empire Magazine, The Denver Post*, July 15, 1973.

"Letters of Nathaniel Hill in Colorado Magazine Tell of Visit To Boulder in 1864; Recall Pioneer Henry Blake." *Boulder Daily Camera*, January 23, 1957.

"Lincoln's Law Partner Became Boulder Resident." *Boulder Daily Camera*, February 12, 1936.

McCoy, Jan. "Boulder's First Churches Reflect the Sturdy Spirit of the Pioneers." *Focus. Boulder Daily Camera*, February 10, 1980.

"Methodists Will Celebrate 75th Anniversary." *Boulder Daily Camera*, November 24, 1934.

"Mrs. Mabel Maxwell Brace, Pioneer, Writes of Early Life in Boulder." (unidentified clipping)

"Mrs. Mary Wood Taylor Writes of Boulder As She Remembers It in Decade, 1889-1899." *Boulder Daily Camera*, March 9, 1959.

Morton, Marlene. "Boulder County's Oldest Cabin." *Town & Country*, October 5, 1967.

O'Brien, Sadie. "Mrs. Emma Beel Reminisces on Boulder 61 Years Ago." *Boulder Daily Camera*, September 31, 1960.

Paddock, Laurence. "Naming the Flatirons." *Focus. Boulder Daily Camera*, July 4, 1976.

Parsons, Martin. "Toll Road History of Boulder County." *Boulder Daily Camera*, July 31, 1945.

"Pioneer Boulder Churches and Their Successors." *Boulder Daily Camera*, November 24, 1934.

Sears, Paul M. "Boulder's Brief Oil Boom." *Empire Magazine. The Denver Post*, March 31, 1968.

Smith, Phyllis. "Old Boulder Sketches Of The Past." *Town & Country*, February 22, March 22, June 28, July 19, July 26, 1978.

"Boettchers Left Indelible Mark on Region." *Rocky Mountain News*, June 17, 1979.

"Territorial Legislator from Boulder County Became Judge." *Boulder Daily Camera*, August 24, 1956.

Veysey, A. E. "Pioneers Planted Wheat in Boulder 75 Years Ago." *The Denver News*, 1935.

Watts, Hugh F. "First 37 Years of Mining in Boulder." *Boulder Daily Camera*, October 29, 1962.

—————. "History of Early Milling in Boulder County," *Boulder Daily Camera*, March 26, 1934.

Wolff, Joseph. "How The First Newspaper Came to Boulder." *Boulder Daily Camera*, February 27, 1908.

Manuscript Collections, Papers.

Boulder, Colorado, University of Colorado Western Historical Collections:

Albion Mining Properties Collection
Andrew, George A. Personal Statement. Bancroft manuscript, 1886.
Arnett, Anthony. Personal Statement. Bancroft manuscript, 1886.
Austin, Eugene A. Personal Statement. Bancroft manuscript, 1886.
Bennett, W. F. Memoirs. 1874-1879.
Brookfield, A.A. Personal Statement. Bancroft manuscript, n.d.
Buckingham Brothers Papers
Church, J.L. Personal Statement. Bancroft manuscript, 1886.
Coffin, O.C. Personal Statement, Bancroft manuscript, 1886.
Collie, Charlotte. Collection. 1884-1906.
Colorado Chautauqua Collection
Culver, Robert. Personal Statement. Bancroft manuscript, 1886 [?]
Davidson, William A. Personal Statement. Bancroft manuscript. 1886.
Drumm, Henry. Autobiographical manuscript.
Dykstra, Anne H. Boulder and the University of Colorado 1861 to 1900. May 6, 1969.
Faurot, C.S. Personal Statement. Bancroft manuscript. 1886.
Fine, Eben G. Collection. 1885-1900.
Fonda, George F. Personal Statement. Bancroft manuscript. 1886.
Fritz, Percy S. Mining in Boulder County.
Fritz, Percy S. Papers.
Gifford, A.D. Personal Statement. Bancroft manuscript. 1886.
Hakes, Steven. A Comparative Survey and Analysis of the Urban Growth Trends of Boulder, Colorado, and Golden, Colorado. 1977.
History of Old Congregational Church Bell. n.d.
Hitchings, John A. Diary. 1849-1911.
Johnson, Arthur C. Papers. 1887-1937.
Leyner, Peter. Personal Statement. Bancroft manuscript. 1886.
Martin, William. Personal Statement. Bancroft manuscript. n.d.
Maxwell, James P. Papers. 1863-1920.
McCammon, Hugh. Personal Statement. Bancroft manuscript. 1886.
McCaslin, N.L. Personal Statement. Bancroft manuscript. 1886.
Meyring, Geneva Todd. Brief History of Nederland. n.d.
Meyring, Henry. Personal Statement. Bancroft manuscript. 1866.
Myers, Arthur E. Eggleston, Kinne, Weston, Willis, Myers, and Murphy families of Boulder County, Colorado.
Nichols, David H. Papers. 1860s-1890s.
Pease, Ernest M. Family Papers. 1863-1943.
Pell, W. G. Personal Statement. Bancroft manuscript. n.d.
Perrigo, Lynn I. A Municipal History of Boulder, 1871-1946.
Pfister, Herbert. Boulder, Colorado, 1880-1920. "The Development from a Frontier Town to a Multifunctional City." 1977.
Place, Eleanor B. History of Boulder, Colorado. 1972.
Potter, R.B. Personal Statement. Bancroft manuscript. 1866.
Rand, George. Personal Statement. Bancroft manuscript. 1866.
Seeley, W.L. Personal Statement. Bancroft manuscript. 1866.
Smith, Marinus. Personal Statement. Bancroft manuscript. 1866.
Spears, Clarence L. Boulder, Colorado in 1883, An Experiment, and a Beginning in Local History.
Stanton, Timothy William. "Eighty Years of Joy and Gladness Mingled with some Work and Sadness." 1860-1953.
Taylor, David C. Personal Statement. Bancroft manuscript. 1886.

Thompson, Nathan. Papers. 1865-1875.
Tyler, Clinton M. Papers. 1860-1886.
Walker, James A. Personal Statement. Bancroft manuscript. 1886.
White, Fred. Personal Statement. Bancroft manuscript. 1886.
Williams, G. Personal Statement. Bancroft manuscript. 1886.
Williams, Thomas. Personal Statement. Bancroft manuscript. 1886.
Williamson, George R. Personal Statement. Bancroft manuscript. n.d.

Books and Pamphlets

Bird, Isabella. *A Lady's Life in the Rocky Mountains*. Norman: University of Oklahoma Press, 1960.
Bixby, Amos. *History of Clear Creek and Boulder Valleys*. Chicago: O.L. Baskin & Co., 1880.
Boulder's Arapaho Glacier. Boulder: Chamber of Commerce, n.d.
Bowles, Samuel. *Our New West*. Hartford: Hartford Publishing Company, 1869.
Coel, Margaret. *Chief Left Hand*. Norman: University of Oklahoma Press, 1981.
Colorado Inventory of Historical Sites. Denver: State Historical Society of Colorado, 1976.
Crossen, Forest. *Anthony Arnett, Empire Builder*. Boulder: 1933.
Fine, Eben. *Remembered Yesterdays*. Boulder: Boulder Historical Society, 1957.
Fritz, Percy S. *The Constitutions and Laws of Early Mining Districts*. Boulder: University of Colorado Studies. Vol. 21, no. 2, March 1934.
Goodwin, Elizabeth F., *The Growth of a Community. Planning and Development: City of Boulder 1859-1966*. Boulder: City Planning Office, 1966.
Goodykoontz, Colin, *First Congregational Church of Boulder, 1864-1939*. Boulder: First Congregational Church, 1939.
Grand Island Mining District, Boulder County, Colorado. 1876.
Greeley, Horace. *Overland Journey to California in 1859*. New York: Saxton, Barker & Co., 1860.
Guide to Boulder's Heritage. Boulder: Department of Community Development, 1976.
Hafen, Le Roy. *Colorado Gold Rush, 1858-59*. Southwest History Series. Vol. 10. Philadelphia: Porcupine Press, 1974.
History of the First Congregational Church of Boulder. Boulder: First Congregational Church, 1979.
Hoover, Frances Montgomery. *Castle o' Montgomery*. Nashville: The Parthenon Press, 1974.
In Boulder. Boulder: Knights of Pythias, 1895.
Julian, Paul. *Wind Study*. Environmental Data Service, 1971.
National State Bank of Boulder 1874-1969. Boulder: National State Bank, 1969.
Native Silver Mining Company of Boulder County, Colo., Caribou, Colo. Prospectus, 1880.
Patton, A.C. *Green Rocks*. 1904.
Pettem, Sylvia. *Red Rocks to Riches*. Boulder: Stonehenge, 1980.
Repplier, F.O. *As A Town Grows*. Boulder: School District No. 3, 1959.
Runnells, Donald D. *Boulder–A Sight To Behold*. Boulder: Johnson Publishing Company, 1976.
Smith, Phyllis. *History of Mapleton School*. Boulder: 1976.
Smith, Phyllis. *A Look at Boulder: From Settlement to City*. Boulder: Pruett Publishing Company, 1981.
Souvenir Boulder, Post Office. McMaster Publishing Co., 1898.
Sturtevant, Joseph Bevier. *Views of Boulder and Vicinity*. 1880.
The Switzerland Trail Guide Book. Denver: The Colorado & Northern Ry., 1904.

Tice, John H. *Over The Plains and Mountains*. St. Louis: St. Louis Book & News
    Co., 1872.

Periodicals

Brown, Abner. "Colorado's First Schools: The First School in Boulder, Colorado."
    Journal of American History. Vol. XV, No. 1, Jan.-Mar. 1921: 72-76.
Kelly, William R. "Irrigation Beginnings in Colorado." *Denver Westerners
    Round-up*. March 1960.
Loyd, Elizabeth. "Matt McCaslin, Sr." *Boulder County Miner*. September 26,
    1912.
"Revolutionary War Widow Owned Boulder Townsite." *Home and Leisure
    Magazine*. March 1970.
"The Historical Story of Boulder." *Saturday Truth*. March 28, 1903.

Public Documents

Boulder, Colorado, University of Colorado Western Historical Collection:

Boulder City Town Company, Records. 1859-1864.
Jackson Land Claim Association. Minutes. 1859-1861.
U.S. Census Reports. Boulder population statistics. 1870-1950.

Letters

Boulder, Colorado, University of Colorado Western Historical Collection:

Adriance, Rev. J. to Rev. John A. Davis. April 14, 1904.
Thompson, Rev. Nathan to *Boulder County News*. Comp. by Sanford Gladden.
    1976.

Notes

The numbers at left of each reference are page numbers.

6. (Aikens' recollection) *Boulder County News*, July 14, 1876.

11. (Bear Head conversation) Amos Bixby, *History of Clear Creek and Boulder Valleys*, 379.

11. (auriferous) *Nebraska Advertiser*, December 9 and 29, 1858, cited in Pettem, *Red Rocks to Riches*, 4.

12. (humbug) Letter, A.A. Brookfield to Emma Brookfield, January 26, 1859, cited in Pettem, *Red Rocks to Riches*, 5.

12. (shot gold) Letter, A.A. Brookfield to Emma Brookfield, February 27, 1859, cited in Hafen, *Colorado Gold Rush, 1858-59, Contemporary Letters and Reports*, 242.

13. (important town) *Nebraska Advertiser*, March 24, 1859, cited in Pettem, *Red Rocks to Riches*, 5.

16. (miners' laws) Percy S. Fritz, *The Constitutions and Laws of Early Mining Districts in Boulder County, Colorado*.

16. (first blood) Percy S. Fritz, "Mining History of Boulder County," *Boulder Daily Camera*, July 31, 1945, supplement.

19. (cabin) Recollections, Mrs. David H. Nichols (Western History Collection, University of Colorado, Boulder).

19. (baking) Ibid., 9.

19. (washing) Ibid., 10.

20. (hamlet) Horace Greeley, *Overland Journey to California in 1859*, 166.

20. (log houses) Letter, Rev. J. Adriance to Rev. John A. Davis, April 14, 1904.

20. (fairy tales) Recollections, Mrs. David H. Nichols, 1.

21. (miner's life) Diary, John A. Hitchings (Western History Collection, University of Colorado, Boulder.)

21. (miner's life) "Letter of Nathaniel Hill. . .," *Boulder Daily Camera*, January 23, 1957.

25. (room) Abner Brown, "Colorado's First Schools: The First School in Boulder," *Journal of American History*, Vol. XV, No. 1, Jan.-Mar. 1921, 72.

26. (purloiner) "First Public School in Colorado Opened in Boulder 75 Years Ago," *Boulder Daily Camera*, October 11, 1935, 7.

27. (pathos) Recollections, Mrs. David H. Nichols, 10.

35. (sweet sleep) Letter, Rev. J. Adriance to Rev. John A. Davis, April 14, 1904.

36. (letter) Colin B. Goodykoontz, *The First Congregational Church of Boulder*, 7.

36. (county seat) Letter, Rev. Nathan Thompson, *Boulder County News*, January 9, 1880.

37. (bell) Goodykoontz, 17.

38. (newspaper) Joseph Woolf, "How The First Newspaper Came To Boulder," *Boulder Daily Camera*, February 27, 1908.

40. (hanging) Joseph Woolf, "Boulder's Only Hanging," *Boulder Daily Camera*, March 26, 1908.

41. (wispy visitors) Linda Cornett, "Boulder's Ghosts," *Focus, Boulder Daily Camera*, October 23, 1977.

42. (Yankee) "Letter of Nathaniel Hill. . ."
42. (first view) Goodykoontz, 7.
43. (winds) Thompson Letter.
43. (Boulder) Samuel Bowles, *Our New West*, 127-8.
51. (mud) *Boulder County News*, December 1, 1871.
54. (brick city) Mrs. M.P. Colburn, *Massachusetts Ploughman*, quoted in *Boulder County News*, October 4, 1872.
54. (beautiful homes) George M. Rice, *Worcester Gazette*, quoted in *Boulder Daily Camera*, September 4, 1892, cited in Perrigo, "A Municipal History of Boulder, 1871-1946," 30.
55. (longest-lived institution) "Boulder Salutes National State Bank," *Boulder Daily Camera*, April 21, 1939.
56. (crazy) Frances Montgomery Hoover, *Castle o' Montgomery*, 105.
57. (Old Main) Jane Sewall, *Jane, Dear Child*, 41.
58. (bull, mud) Oscar E. Jackson, "History of the University," *The Columbine*, Vol. 1, May 1, 1883, cited in Dykstra, "Boulder and the University of Colorado, 1861 to 1900," 5.
58. (our beautiful town) *Denver Daily Times*, March 30, 1875.
59. (fogies) *Boulder County Herald*, December 7, 1881, both cited in Perrigo, 14.
59. (grasshoppers) Brown, 75.
60. (Bolton) Forest Crossen, "O.C. Bolton Recalls Earlier Days of Farm Life in Boulder," *Boulder Daily Camera*, n.d. (Western History Collection, University of Colorado, Boulder.)
61. (happiest years) John Swagerty, "Boettchers Left Indelible Mark on Region," *Rocky Mountain News*, June 17, 1979.
63. (carpets) Sanford G. Gladden, "Boulder's First Hotel," *Boulder Daily Camera*, August 2, 1970.
64. (Lincoln) "Lincoln's Law Partner Became Boulder Resident," *Boulder Daily Camera*, February 12, 1936.
66. (Jesse James) Forest Crossen, "Jesse James' Visit in Boulder Was Recalled by Son of Hosts," *Boulder Daily Camera*, August 14, 1965.
67. (raw edge) F.O. Repplier, *As A Town Grows*.
74. (studio of nature) Harrington, *Summering in Colorado*, cited in Perrigo, 23.
74. (Sanitarium) *Brief History/Boulder, Colorado Sanitarium*, 1.
74. (Chautauqua) *The Texas-Colorado Chautauqua*, 1.
79. (traitors) *Boulder Daily Camera*, July 28, 1891, cited in Perrigo, 19.
79. (payroll) *Boulder Daily Camera*, November 27, 1895, cited in Dykstra, 8.
80. (unbridged creek) Letter, Rev. Nathan Thompson, *Boulder County News*, January 9, 1880.

Index